How to Win at Classroom Management in 6 Easy Steps

Angie Barrett

Pembroke Publishers Limited

Dedicated to all the teachers who have ever thought: I can't do this. You can and I'll show you how.

© 2026 Pembroke Publishers
538 Hood Road
Markham, Ontario, Canada L3R 3K9
www.pembrokepublishers.com

All rights reserved.
No part of this publication may be reproduced in any form or by any means electronic or mechanical, including photocopy, scanning, recording, or any information, storage or retrieval system, including Artificial Intelligence, without permission in writing from the publisher. Excerpts from this publication may be reproduced under licence from Access Copyright, or with the express written permission of Pembroke Publishers Limited, or as permitted by law.

Every effort has been made to contact copyright holders for permission to reproduce borrowed material. The publishers apologize for any such omissions and will be pleased to rectify them in subsequent reprints of the book.

Library and Archives Canada Cataloguing in Publication

Title: How to win at classroom management in 6 easy steps / Angie Barrett.

Other titles: How to win at classroom management in six easy steps

Names: Barrett, Angie, author.

Description: Includes bibliographical references and index.

Identifiers: Canadiana (print) 20260100471 | Canadiana (ebook) 2026010048X | ISBN 9781551383750 (softcover) | ISBN 9781551389790 (PDF)

Subjects: LCSH: Classroom management.

Classification: LCC LB2013 .B37 2026 | DDC 371.102/4—dc23

Editor: David Kilgour
Cover Design: John Zehethofer
Typesetting: Jay Tee Graphics Ltd.

Printed and bound in Canada
9 8 7 6 5 4 3 2 1

Contents

Introduction: Step into the World of Teaching

No matter if you're entering a kindergarten, a grade 5, or a grade 12 classroom, they all have very similar characteristics. I'll go into more detail about those characteristics shortly but believe it or not all students in your care, no matter their age, require clear, high expectations, follow-through on consequences, and compassion. I believe every teacher can pull something from the pages of this book that will help them manage a space full of people. We are all very familiar with the idea of classroom management and the many challenges that come with it. It's extremely difficult to herd, then lead, a group of individuals who all come with their own stories, voices, experiences, opinions, traumas, goals, and, yes, baggage. Students are three-dimensional humans rather than empty vessels waiting for our infinite wisdom to be poured in. They come to us as unique, gifted, flawed, three-dimensional humans who deserve respect, appreciation, empathy, compassion, and validation as well as guidance, consequences, and consistency.

I've organized this book in the same way I organize my life, with chaotic good intentions. You'll see each of my "six easy steps" separated into sections of varying lengths within which you'll find an array of information, stories, templates, tips, and tricks as well as strategies that you can try tomorrow.

While I've gone to the trouble of creating my own templates and samples for you to use, you may find that using AI is quicker and easier. I know, I know, there's a lot of controversy around using AI in both the teaching world and the publishing world. I'm going to come right out and lay my truth on the table. I love AI! I think, for teachers especially, it has so much potential to make our workloads lighter. You can use it for templates and samples, as I've suggested, for lists and how tos, for diagrams, and even for feedback, lesson, and unit planning. Of course, when using a technology such as this, we need to do so with the intention of adapting whatever we create with the help of AI to the needs of the students we have in front of us. It must be personalized to our classes.

I also love AI for student use...which I know are fighting words to some. I can see so many ways we can use AI to help students with critical thinking, resource analysis, organization, and creative thinking/innovation. AI isn't going away and it will get better and more powerful, so I believe we should teach students how to use it ethically and responsibly. But that, my friends, is a whole other book.

You chose teaching for any number of reasons. Maybe you were born to be a teacher. Maybe you dreamed of being a teacher since you were little. Maybe, like me, you stumbled into it. With teaching comes many perks. We get summers off. We have great pensions (in Canada). We get holidays through the school year. We get paid pretty well (don't get me started about cost-of-living adjustments). We have health benefits. We inspire other, younger humans and change their lives. Sometimes we even save their lives (thank you, past self, for taking a first-aid course). For thirty years or so, we're in it. While we're in it, we might aspire to leadership roles and mentoring stints, moving up the chain of command to become vice-principals, principals, consultants, or even directors of education.

No matter where you end up, I guarantee, you started with excitement, thrilled to have a job, over the moon to be in front of students and in your own classroom. You were grateful to be employed in a fairly stable career with a purpose beyond the average kind of work: you were going to inspire our youth to be the most they could be. Please remember that grateful excitement. It's essential for those reading who might be old pros at this teacher stuff but might also be struggling a bit with classroom management and also for those new teachers who have had the shine wear off the new job. Disillusionment usually comes knocking early on in our careers and it can make us forget how excited we once were.

The times may have changed but the needs of students haven't.

Achieving mastery over classroom management can look like a lot of work. I'm not going to lie: it is. But it's work that doesn't have to be done and dusted in a week, month, or year. It can take your entire career to figure it all out. You're in it, after all, for thirty plus, so take your time in using my suggestions and ideas. Return to this book and reread parts. Tackle one step at a time.

Although I recommend reading this book in sequential order, there are parts, with strategies, that you can skip if you're not entirely ready to tackle them at this time in your career. I've highlighted sidenotes in their own boxes to identify important and quick tips and/or information, and each of the centre chapters ends with an overview of key points for quick reference.

While I can't promise that after reading my book you'll never have any challenges in your classrooms, I can say this: I've been an educator for twenty years. I've seen it, lived it, and tested many strategies to both success and failure. I've had challenging classes and students who have really tried my patience. I've dreaded walking into rooms and have contemplated throwing my hands up and quitting. I've also mentored teachers through similar struggles. I've rescued some from unsuccessful evaluations. I know what needs to be done to ensure the best environment for all people involved and I can teach it to you in six easy steps.

STEP 1

Understand the Power Players and How They Work

There are three power players in every classroom:

- The *Environment* (the classroom itself),
- The *Students,*
  and
- *You.*

Power Player One: The Environment

No place is neutral.

No place is neutral. Every space has its own baggage. It holds connotations. It has a vibe. If you loathe cooking with a passion, then walking into a kitchen to prepare an elaborate meal for hungry people every single day is going to be a struggle. Even if it's your job, you may not put your heart and soul into it. Sometimes, you may even get quite snarly about it.

As humans, we tend to generalize our strong emotions about things. If you've had a really terrible experience at an amusement park, like going on a couple of rides that used to be loads of fun, yanking your spine in ways you didn't think possible, then projectile-vomiting in front of a large crowd of waiting riders (true story), you'll likely not want to go back again.

The same space can feel like home and joy to one person and like a prison and torture to another. It shouldn't be any shock to learn that some students feel both ways about classrooms, which is why it's so important to adequately consider the space you're preparing for them.

The room itself might be one that students have been in before. It might remind them of other rooms they've been in, or seen on TV or online. If they've had emotions in a space — high, low, bad, good — then that space, and all like it, can develop a loaded meaning unique to them. They can carry assumptions into those rooms based on their past experiences. And, attached to those assumptions, are emotions.

If Rebecca was teased relentlessly at school last year, in her very classroom no less, then she may associate that kind of space with fear, anger, and helplessness.

Added to the expectations and *emotions* students bring with them, classrooms may have been built decades ago or may have just opened, which means they may or may not have amenities that make the space comfortable, like air conditioning or adequate ventilation. The space might be the very same space in the exact same building that our students' parents or siblings were taught in. Students may have heard countless stories about things that have happened in these rooms, things that have nothing to do with you because you weren't even there but that nonetheless have tremendous impact on the assumptions and emotions students carry into the room.

Even the hallway to get to the room can have profound impact. Imagine if every time you walked a certain path to your destination, you were bullied. It happens in school hallways all the time. Comments get flung, physical contact happens, supervision is not always present, thereby allowing terrifying things to happen. These things can make a student feel very unsafe even before they make it to their classroom which, in turn, can dysregulate them in so many different ways. You might not even realize they're dysregulated because they may seem okay on the surface but inside their emotions are writhing and reeling.

My point is, students will walk into these rooms with expectations, assumptions, biases, emotions and so will you because, in all likelihood, you've also had experiences in rooms like the one you're attempting to make community in.

These rooms also represent the institution of education which evolved with industrialization, and which perpetuates the same core beliefs as it did when it was created over one hundred years ago. It embodies a one-size-fits-all model of late 19th- and early 20th-century social reform and was built on foundations that aimed for social cohesion at the expense of individuation. Education, as it now exists, is built on a foundation that is inherently flawed due to interwoven oppression that existed from the very beginning and persists to current times with barriers that impact all who enter the space, some more profoundly than others. And those barriers, which we as teachers have been indoctrinated into accepting through years of education, can be unseen by us even though they negatively impact the success of many of our students.

Education, as it now exists, is built on a foundation that is inherently flawed.

What I'm trying to say is that the space that you're working in, where you're teaching, carries deep, impactful meaning in a plethora of ways, some invisible to you and out of your control, but some very much in your domain of influence.

What this means is, if you want to win at classroom management, it is *vital* that you set up a space that is safe and welcoming for every human who enters it.

If possible, before you even step foot in such a space, you're going to need: A vision.

Strategy: Developing a Vision for Your Classroom

A vision embodies your expectations for a space and requires some level of honest self-reflection.

Ask yourself:

- What does my classroom look like?
  - Do I have inspirational/comedic/instructional pictures up?
  - Is there a theme? Is it corny? Cool? Contemporary? Traditional?
  - Do I have student work decorating a wall? More than one wall?

Hint: You should definitely have student work somewhere on display no matter the grade — and not just the work that "makes the cut". This shows your students that their work is valuable and also provides examples of the diversity of thinking, creativity, and experience in your classroom.

- How does the space serve the needs of everyone who enters?
  - Can students move around freely?
  - How do you arrange the tables/desks/chairs?
  - Where is the teacher desk?
  - Are there areas designed for different purposes? A reading area? A chill spot? A teacher conference space?

Hint: Obviously, you have to work with the space you have as well as with the furniture available and whatever support your administration gives you, but even with desks, chairs, and four walls, you can still make the space feel like a home. If you're stuck on what that looks like, try asking your students what they'd like a classroom to be like and co-create a room organization that works for all of you.

*This could be an excellent get-to-know-you activity, by the way, and would help students feel a sense of ownership and pride over the space.

  - Where are *you* for most of the class time?

Hint: For the love of chocolate, please do not spend the entire class sitting at your desk. Part of successful classroom management is working the room. Teach from everywhere in the space at one point or another. Yes, I know you have marking that needs to get done and you will have time to do it (I'll get to that later) but you must work the room daily. Get your steps in! If you have mobility restrictions, try to position yourself in the middle of the room and, if possible, in a chair that moves so you can swivel and make eye contact/put eyes on everyone.

  - Where do you put the agenda? Students need a clear understanding of what they will be doing (and why), in what order, and for how long.
  - Do you have an upcoming assignment calendar? Homework for the day reminders?

Hint: Please, do not, *ever*, make a public list of students who have not completed work or who have misbehaved. Public shaming will not create a safe space for students to learn. It hurts them and obliterates their trust in you.

  - Are there checklists for daily routines/goals/tasks?

Hint: Breaking tasks down into short/workable goals (chunking) is a helpful strategy for everyone and being able to mark things off a list as done is very satisfying; it also provides a model for students to organize time in manageable ways.

We can't assume that students know cell phones are not allowed.

- Is there a sign-out log for washroom trips? Where? On the board? By the door? Discreet is better, in my opinion.
- Depending on the grade, where do the cell phones go? Will you be using them in a lesson at times? Be clear about cell-phone use expectations from day one. In fact, I advise creating a short list of expectations to send home before the first day of class so that families are aware of what you want to see immediately when students enter the room.
  - To parents: "In order to have everyone's full attention on creating a community and, since we won't be using cell phones for any introduction activities, I'm asking all students to have their phones put away in bags or lockers before entering class."
  - No need to say more than that up front. Guidelines and rules can be nailed down in more detail once students are in the space. I remind students as I'm welcoming them, to make sure they put their phones away. "I don't want to see them today." Then, once we get settled, I explain why we won't be using cell phones in class, when we might use them, and what the consequences will be for taking one out without permission.
- Who is the focal point of the space?

Hint: If the focus is you, then please rethink that. The space isn't about you, it's about your students. We are in service of our students. Everything we do should be to help them learn, grow, and succeed. While you may absolutely love *Star Wars* or *Minions* or Taylor Swift, and you want to share that obsession with your students, there must be room for them to share their obsessions too.

- Reflection should include visualizing what you want the classroom, with all students in attendance, to look, feel, smell, and sound like.
  - What vibe are you going for? What message will your vibe send to students? Staff? Admin? Parents?
  - How do you want your students to feel in the space?
  - Will you allow eating during class time? If so, what food restrictions will there be beyond the obvious allergenic ones? Do you want to avoid super smelly or noisy foods during instruction/work time? Do you want to allow water only? Or small, quiet snacks? Will you have snacks available for students who need them? Does the school provide snacks?
  - Will you co-create behavior expectations with your students? Will you post those expectations somewhere so they're visible or will they be virtual in an online classroom? Whatever you decide, they need to exist somewhere for students, families, you, supply teachers, etc. to refer to.

Write in a journal, brainstorm, mind-map, doodle, make a list, create a collage, get some thoughts down about your ideal classroom, with the understanding that no matter how well you plan, you also need the patience and flexibility to alter course because anything can change despite your best efforts to control it. You could be assigned a different room at the last minute. You might end up having a different teaching assignment. You might be sharing a room with another teacher or working in a common area because there are no classrooms left (like the cafeteria or library). There might be a change in board or school policy that impacts some of your beliefs about how the space should be used.

No matter what may come your way, you do need some idea of your expectations for the space, any space you're in, so that you show consistency.

Consistency, reliability, is a fundamental need for every student.

Consistency, reliability, is a fundamental need for every student you encounter.

"Mr. Alin's classroom is so chill. He lets us sit where we want when we're working. We can't leave without asking though, and we have to write the time we leave and come back in the logbook by the door. He's pretty strict about that."

"Miss Ellis always starts class with a riddle on the whiteboard for us to do. Then she walks around to everyone's desk and checks our homework to make sure we know what we're doing. If we don't, she goes over things with us again."

"We always read first thing when class starts. Even our teacher reads!"

"Carpet time is quiet time."

"Mrs. Abby wants us to sit in our home groups when she's teaching and we are never allowed to have our phones out."

Everything you do, as much as possible, should be planned and, if you need to change the plan, you must explain to students why and how. Change is hard. We all know this, so we can't expect our students to be okay with change when it comes with no explanation. Sometimes the explanation is simply, "This seating plan isn't working for everyone so I designed a new one for us to try out."

That being said, making change just to shake students up on a regular basis is not a great idea. I've seen teachers switch up seating plans weekly so that students stay "on their toes" but what this actually does is creates unnecessary stress. Also, you may (likely do) have students who are neurodivergent and who may struggle in profound (sometimes silent, agonizing) ways when change happens suddenly. You need to know your students well enough to ensure safety for everyone, even when it comes to changing things in the space.

I'm not saying you can't use seating plans as part of your classroom management repertoire (more on this later), but don't create chaos just to mess with your students. If you unsettle the space too often, it's not going feel like a safe space.

We have enough chaos coming our way on the daily. There are thousands of on-the-spot decisions to make on any given school day. We need a solid understanding, a foundation of what we want our classroom to be like, knowing, of course, that we will adapt to suit the needs of our students as we get to know them. So we need to plan ahead.

Note: Students will judge you harshly for being consistently unorganized. Ironic, I know.

Note: Having a plan for the space (among all the other things you do to prepare, execute, then reflect) goes a long way in letting students know that *you* know what you're doing. They must feel confident that they can rely on you to know what's going on. If you don't know what's going on, then you can tell them that you'll figure it out and get back to them. Consistency and organization equal competence in the eyes of students and competence equals a sense of safety.

And that, my friends, builds trust.

One of my mandates when I got hired as a librarian at my current school was to transform the library from a stuffy, quiet, poorly utilized space into a social hub. I wanted it to be a safe and welcoming environment. I had a vision of a space that was filled with students, working, playing, socializing, reading, and learning. I knew it would be loud and unconventional. I knew students would get out of hand at times. I also knew I'd be able to manage it with some pre-planning and well-thought-out expectations.

I weeded hundreds of old books out of the collection so I could take down shelves and make more room for students to hang out. I brought in games and cards, crafts and puzzles. I organized furniture to maximize room for play and room for study. I allow eating (just as I have always done in my classrooms) because being hungry doesn't mesh well with mood stabilization or concentration. I remind students of my expectations about cleanliness and appropriate behavior. The books I buy are current and coveted. One of my greatest joys is seeing a student get so excited about a book that they jump up and down, squeal with excitement, then hug the book. It's the best thing ever to witness!

On any given day, at peak times, I have at least a hundred plus students in the space and I've been repeatedly told by students, parents, and staff that the library is the best space in the whole school. The favorite place. A safe space.

How did I accomplish this? I applied the same principles to the library as I always have to my classrooms.

Here are some templates to help you design a space that works for you *and* your students.

Developing a Space with a Vision — Teacher Version

Purpose: To create a safe and welcoming community space.

Developing My Classroom Vision

- What is the first reaction students should have when they walk into our classroom?
- What feelings should our classroom inspire (welcoming, comfortable, fun, exciting)?
- If our classroom could speak, what would it say to every student?

Vibe

- List 3–5 words that describe how I want our classroom community to be (e.g., respectful, creative, fun, peaceful).
- How can I convey this vibe with colors, images, and/or words?
  - How will students have voice in the classroom?
  - How will cultures and identities be present?
  - How will I adapt to students' needs and interests?

Function

- How will I first set up the room with the furniture that's available? (Consider: group work, independent work, recharge spaces.)

Next Steps for My Vision

- **Three actions I can take right now** to shape my classroom toward my vision:
  1. ______________________________
  2. ______________________________
  3. ______________________________
- **One pie-in-the-sky wish for my classroom:**

  ____

  ____

Developing a Space with a Vision — Student Version

Why are we doing this?

It's important to me that everyone feels welcome and safe in our classroom. I'd love to learn what you like, dislike, would keep, or would change in our classroom.

- When I first walked into our classroom I felt:
- Tell me 3 words that you wish our classroom made you feel more of:
  1. ____________________
  2. ____________________
  3. ____________________

Vibe

- What can we do to make sure everyone feels like they belong and are safe here?

  ____

  ____
- What would you like to see more of around the room? (posters, colors, decorations, books, etc)?

  ____

  ____
- What things would you like to see less of around the room?

  ____

  ____

I Learn Best When…

- The classroom is (use descriptive words like happy, exciting, calm, quiet, loud):

  ____

  ____

Our Classroom Community

- How do we practice respect and kindness in our classroom?

  ____

  ____

  ____

One Wish

One wish I have for our classroom is:

____

____

Pembroke Publishers ©2026 *How to Win at Classroom Management in 6 Easy Steps* by Angie Barrett ISBN 978-1-55138-375-0

Co-Creating Our Vision

1. Compare your reflection with your students' reflections.
2. Sort out the common themes/ideas (comfortable, calm, fun, creative).
3. As a class, develop a **Vision Statement**. It can start with:
   Our classroom will…
4. Post the statement where students and visitors will see it.

Developing a Space with a Vision — Sample Teacher & Student Version

(This is my version. Yours will probably differ.)

Building a Classroom Space with Purpose & Belonging

Part 1: Teacher Reflection — My Classroom Vision
Clarifying My Vision

- What is the first reaction students should have when they walk into our classroom?
  A sense of calm, safety, and purpose—where expectations are clear and curiosity is encouraged.
- What feelings should our classroom inspire?
  Welcomed, respected, confident, ready to learn, safe, reassured, and engaged.
- If our classroom could speak, what would it say to every student?
  "You belong here. Your ideas matter. This is a place to learn, try, and grow."

Vibe

- List 3–5 words that describe how I want our classroom community to be:
  1. *Inclusive*
  2. *Respectful*
  3. *Curious/creative*
  4. *Supportive/collaborative*
  5. *Thought-provoking*
- How can I convey this vibe with colors, images and/or words?
  - *Student work and thinking (works-in-progress, not just polished pieces, samples, questions, ideas)*
  - *Clear routines and expectations (Co-constructed guidelines)*
  - *Diverse learning materials, images, and examples*
  - *Classroom library with variety and inclusivity*
  - *Fluid seating*
  - *Me, happy to see them*
- How will I give students voice in the classroom?
  - *Student-created displays*
  - *Multicultural texts and visuals*
  - *Opportunities for students to share interests, traditions, and ideas*
- How will cultures and identities be present?
  Through shared guidelines, inclusive language, and visible representation of student identities and voices. Wide array of texts, selected with an anti-oppressive lens and formatted in accessible ways including audio, graphics, video, etc., student-created

work on display, co-created guidelines posted. Student-crafted "get-to-know-me" and celebration activities on display.

- How will I adapt to students' needs and interests?
  Displays and layouts will change based on learning goals, student needs, and feedback. Revisit co-constructed guidelines, tweaking as needed.

Function

- How will I first set up the room with the furniture that's available?
  Desks will be arranged in groups of 4–6 to work with collaborative activities and small-group discussion and will be moved to accommodate different needs. Desks to the wall, chairs in a circle for discussion. Desks facing each other for paired work.
- Work independently?
  Quiet desks, nooks, or clearly defined focus areas. Alternative seating like a couch or comfy chair. High tables and study carrel for independent work.
- Recharge or self-regulate?
  A calm corner with soft seating, visuals, or self-regulation tools. Station with calming/reset activities which is free to use when needed/no judgement and filled with: fidget toys, coloring pages, markers, pencil crayons, sudoku, word searches, etc. Use of ear pods/headphones for music/podcasts, etc.

Where do I go from here?

- **Three actions I can take right now** to shape my classroom toward my vision:
  1. Rearrange seating to support collaboration and focus.
  2. Replace teacher-only displays with student work.
  3. Introduce routines that build ownership of the space.
- **One pie-in-the-sky wish for my classroom:**
  Students independently caring for and shaping the classroom environment.

Part 2: Student Reflection — Our Classroom Vision

First Impressions

- **When I first walked into our classroom I felt:**
- *Safe, comfortable, seen, and heard*
  Tell me 3 words that you wish our classroom made you feel more of:
  1. *Relaxed*
  2. *Fun*
  3. *Quiet times*

Pembroke Publishers ©2026 *How to Win at Classroom Management in 6 Easy Steps* by Angie Barrett ISBN 978-1-55138-375-0 

Vibe

- What can we do to make sure everyone feels like they belong and are safe here?
  Be kind, listen to each other, and include everyone
- What would you like to see more of around the room?
  Student work, class goals, guidelines, and pictures or words that represent everyone
- What things would you like to see less of around the room?
  Bullying, disrespect, or distractions that make learning hard

I Learn Best When…

- **The classroom is:**
  Calm, organized, and supportive
- **A space where I can focus and work independently looks like:**
  Quiet areas with clear expectations and minimal distractions
- **A space where we can work together looks like:**
  Tables or groups where we can talk, share ideas, and help each other, sit with friends or at least one friend and get to know others

Our Classroom Community

- How do we practice respect and kindness in our classroom?
  Listening, taking turns, and treating people kindly. Being open-minded and trying not to judge. Sharing, being kind and supporting each other

One Wish

- One wish I have for our classroom is:
  More student choices and cozy learning spaces. More couches!

Part 3: Co-Creating Our Vision

- Compare your reflection with your students' reflections.
  Sharing respect, giving choice, being flexible, helping one another, comfortable spaces, showcase student work, listening, allowing voice
- Sort out the common themes/ideas (e.g., comfortable, calm, fun, creative).
  Organization, respect, choice, kindness, understanding, belonging, fun, quiet
- As a class, develop a **Vision Statement.**
  Our classroom door is open, we welcome one another with kindness, understanding, and a willingness to learn.
- Post the statement where students and visitors will see it.

Pembroke Publishers ©2026 *How to Win at Classroom Management in 6 Easy Steps* by Angie Barrett ISBN 978-1-55138-375-0 

"Chunking"

The concept of chunking things into manageable steps can baffle the best of us, but it's an invaluable tool in classroom management, so I thought I'd provide samples of some ways to chunk information so it's more digestible and doable for students. The reason why I like these samples in particular is because they show teachers how to break down a task, an activity, and a lesson. You can use chunking to break a task into a "to-do" list or an activity into a series of steps and you can make a student-friendly agenda for a block of time for a particular subject. You can also add what students should do if they get their work done before everyone else and what they'll do if they don't get their work done in the time given. Don't forget, you can always use AI to help you chunk existing lessons too.

Sample 1: Chunked Student Work (Grade 5 Math — Word Problems)

Task: Solve and explain a multi-step word problem.
Problem Example:
A bubble gum machine has 325 gumballs. We go to the bulk store and buy 178 more gumballs to add to the machine. Then 96 gumballs are purchased by a few happy gum chewers. How many gumballs are in the bubble gum machine now?

5–7 minutes → Break the problem into parts. I would write each step on the board as well as verbally go through each step with students participating and me circulating to check on progress:

- **First, highlight or underline the key numbers:** 325, 178, 96.
- **Next, identify the question you'll need to answer:** *How many gumballs are in the bubble gum machine now?*
- **Then, follow the steps**:
  - Add the bulk store gumballs we bought.
  - Subtract gumballs that were purchased.

3–5 minutes → Students work on first step while I move around the room, checking on progress and giving feedback/encouragement:

- Solve the addition:

  325
  \+ 178
  ———
  503

3–5 minutes → Students work on second step while I move around the room, checking on progress and giving feedback/encouragement:

- Solve the subtraction:

  503
  \- 96
  ———
  407

Pembroke Publishers ©2026 *How to Win at Classroom Management in 6 Easy Steps* by Angie Barrett ISBN 978-1-55138-375-0

5–10 minutes → Students explain how they got to their answer.

- Instructions on board and verbally: Write down or share with your seat partner how you got to your answer. Use transition words like first, then, finally. *First, I added 325 and 178 to find how many gumballs we had after the we bought more. Then, I subtracted 96 to find how many gumballs were left after some were purchased. Finally, I reached the answer and it is 407 gumballs.*

5 minutes → Students check their work.

- Ask your seat partner: *Does my answer make sense?* If it doesn't make sense, go into detective mode and see if you can work together to find the problem.

Sample 2: Chunked Student Work (Grade 9 Science — Ecology)

Task: Answer a short-response science question with evidence and explanation.
Problem Example (written on board & spoken verbally):
Question: How might introducing wolves into a forest ecosystem affect the populations of deer and plants?

10 minutes → Steps 1 & 2: Understand the question.

- Step 1: Highlight keywords: *wolves, forest ecosystem, deer, plants*
- Step 2: Restate the question in your own words:
  For example: *If wolves are added, what happens to deer and plant numbers?*

10 minutes → Step 3: Gather science ideas from teacher-led and individual research.

(Students can write notes or verbally share learning with a partner.) Teacher will circulate around the room giving encouragement and feedback.

- *Wolves are predators → they eat deer.*
- *Fewer deer → less grazing on plants.*
- *More plants can grow.*
- *Example of "trophic cascade".*

15 minutes → Step 4: Write your answer in short answer form as in the example below.

Sample Student Response:
When wolves are introduced, the deer population goes down because wolves hunt them. With fewer deer eating plants, the plant population increases. This is an example of a trophic cascade, where changes at the top of the food chain affect lower levels.

10 minutes → Step 5: Add details to enhance response using teacher feedback.

- Remember to add specific science vocabulary: *predator-prey relationship, population, ecosystem balance.* (*Write these terms on the board and prompt students to check them as you circulate)
- Revised Sample Response :
  When wolves are introduced into a forest ecosystem, the deer population decreases due to predator-prey interactions. With fewer deer, plants are not eaten as much, so their population increases. This shows a trophic cascade, where one species affects the balance of an entire ecosystem.

5 minutes → Step 6: Students check over their work.

- Did I answer the whole question? (*Yes: wolves, deer, plants, population.*)
- Did I use science terms? (*Predator-prey, population, trophic cascade.*)
- Is my explanation clear? (*Yes.*)

Pembroke Publishers ©2026 *How to Win at Classroom Management in 6 Easy Steps* by Angie Barrett ISBN 978-1-55138-375-0 

Sample 3: Grade 8 Language — Today's Agenda

*Teachers: Instructions that have a sequence (first, next, then) should be written on the board, then referred to as a reminder as work is being done. As the class finishes, cross out or put a check next to the completed steps. This models how to complete work using a sequence of steps and ends with a satisfying checkmark or line through to show completion. Done!
Goal: Today we will learn to write a strong paragraph with evidence and explanation.

10 minutes → Warm-Up

First: Quick Write: Answer this question in your notebook:

*What makes a character likable? *List a characteristic we've learned and tell me why that characteristic makes the character likable.*

Second: Share one idea with a partner.

15 minutes → Mini-Lesson

Learning: What makes a strong paragraph? (Ask students to identify parts of a paragraph as you guide them through the learning.)

- Topic sentence
- Evidence (a quote or detail)
- Explanation (your thinking)
- Concluding sentence

Look at one sample paragraph together and identify the parts.

10 minutes → Practice Time!

Your Turn (with teacher and/or seat partner support):

- First: Write **a topic sentence about one of the characteristics you believe shows likability.**
- Second: Find **one piece of evidence** from a movie or book that shows the characteristic that makes the character likable.

15 minutes → Keep practicing, but this time on your own.

Write a full paragraph on your own.

- First: Choose a different characteristic that makes a character likable.
- Next: Write your paragraph. Be sure to include: topic sentence, evidence, explanation, conclusion.

*Teacher will check in and give feedback while you write.

5 minutes → Wrap-Up

- Share one sentence with your seat partner (if you feel like it, share with the class).
- Ticket Out the Door: What's one thing to remember about writing paragraphs?
  - By the end of class, you'll have written **a complete paragraph with evidence.**

Pembroke Publishers ©2026 *How to Win at Classroom Management in 6 Easy Steps* by Angie Barrett ISBN 978-1-55138-375-0 

We want a system in place so students can come and go with a shared understanding of teacher expectations and school and/or board protocol. We also want to be able to track where students are in case there's an emergency and we need to account for all students. This is a template that I use with great success.

Sign-Out Log: One In, One Out

Name:	Time Out	Time In	Teacher Initials	Notes

In Short

- No space is neutral. Every step a student and teacher takes both inside and outside of a school building can be loaded with experiences, biases, systemic barriers, causes for tears and for smiles. Be sure to understand how that fact can shape the atmosphere of a teaching space.
- You need to develop a vision for your learning space. Consider it a theme or vibe for the room(s). This should be done in advance with the understanding that you'll need to be flexible with the reality of the space you land in. It should be done with your students' well-being at the centre of your plans and should allow for voice, experience, and some element of control for students.
- Your topmost goal for any space you share with students is that it be safe, welcoming, and flexible.

Power Player Two: Students

It is more important than the curriculum, more important than your lesson plan, more important than breathing, that you know your students and that your students know each other. Knowing your students is the most vital aspect of classroom management and it requires more time than any other thing you do as a teacher.

The first week of class, at least, should be devoted to learning about your students and your students learning about each other and, to some extent, about you.

Getting to know your students is vital.

In the first month, you should continue with getting-to-know-you activities, conversations, and observations in meaningful, inclusive, and transparent ways.

In fact, the *entire* time you are teaching a particular cohort of students, there should be mindful actions on your part to continue get to know them.

If you do nothing else, please make sure you do this. I promise you, it is the *one* thing that will make or break your success in classroom management.

Types of Students

Every classroom, of any grade, tends to have a mixture of "kinds of people". I'm not saying it's a great idea to label your students in neat categories. Each one of them has a unique personality and needs a strategic plan of action suited just to them. But as humans, a species that students do fall into, we tend to behave in certain ways, especially in places that are highly regulated by societal expectations. School is a place where patterns of behaviors develop and we find those patterns of behavior in every grade. In fact, what I'm about to go through next might be familiar to you because it also likely exists in your workplace, especially if you work with fifteen or more people.

In any classroom, you will typically encounter the following:

- Studious Humans: very serious students who are keen to please the teacher and be the best at everything they do.
- Nervous/Shy Humans: reluctant to join large group discussions but will work well in small groups. May never speak, for any reason, in a voice more than a whisper or at all.

- Energetic Humans: can't-sit-in-their-seats, aching for leadership, very into competition, sports, and/or games/gaming.
- Performer Humans: want all attention, at all times, good and/or bad.
- Silently Struggling Humans: dejected, feeling hopeless, quiet, often overlooked, usually monosyllabic and mysterious.

Within all of these types of humans you'll find intersectionality and overlapping traits. You'll have days where everyone seems on the same page with you and with each other. Other days, not so much. You'll have students who would rather not participate in any activity unless it's specific to their interests. Who do homework and who don't. Who procrastinate and who hand things in early. You'll have criers and yellers. Sleepers and balls of energy. You'll have students with great privilege and those who face systemic barriers and some who experience both at the same time. You'll have students with special needs and accommodations and those who don't have official documentation but who would benefit from adjustments anyway. You will have many students with anxiety.

You'll also have students, probably not many, but some, who have personalities that are hard to like. They may be "too much" in one way or another, or "off" in some way, or they may have traits that clash very hard with your own and those of everyone else they encounter. They usually don't follow social norms and might actually be quite mean to you and others. It happens. As I said, we're dealing with humans here.

Accepting students just as they are is a really important step in the getting-to-know-you process.

You don't have to like every student you teach. You do, however, have to act as if you like them, or at least, that you accept them just as they are.

On average, on any given school day, you'll have all of these humans in the space you've created and you'll be able to expect, with very few missteps, how things will go because human behavior in educational settings is mostly predictable.

BUT…

Every once in a while. Maybe every other year, maybe every semester, maybe more than that because you're very lucky, there will be a human who is a complete and total *wild card.*

The Wild Card

This kind of student is one you don't see coming. This type of student might be outgoing and charming or quiet and aloof. They might be super popular or a social pariah. They might be a bully or be bullied. They will certainly come with a reputation and you will likely be told *all* about them from colleagues, school records, and even Admin. They are world-weary and old souls and they can see right through you.

These are the students who can change the entire dynamic of your plans and the atmosphere in the classroom.

While all students have layers and complexities, the wild cards are the ones who also, intuitively, know how to dominate any environment they step into.

And they're the ones you need to do the most work to get onside. They're the ones who need the most compassion, patience, and empathy and the most clear, concise, straightforward expectations.

And they will push your limits on all of the above.

One way to deal with a wild card — and I'm just going to come right out and say it — the *wrong*, but most common way, is to isolate them, to use your influence as the "authority figure" to attempt to harness the power of peer pressure to turn the other students against the wild card. If you do this, and I've seen it happen over and over, you're effectively throwing down a gauntlet and starting a war. You've shown your fear and the wild card will take that and use it against you.

It will be very hard, probably impossible, to get your class back after that. All trust will be broken. The safety of the room destroyed.

Years ago, a close friend of mine had a student I'll call Preston. Preston was enigmatic, charismatic, and mischievous. He wasn't into doing homework or completing assignments on time, but he was very, very smart. He had horrendous attendance but when he was present, he was energetic and enthusiastic — usually. He could carry a class discussion and make a lesson the best it could be. And, when his mood carried him, he would also, unapologetically, derail a lesson if it didn't suit him. He could also be volatile. Was incredibly difficult. Questioned everything and would not, under any circumstances, do something just because he was told to. He needed to know why and if the answer wasn'tsensible to him, he simply would not comply. He had so much sway that if he wasn't working, no one else would be.

Preston was a wild card.

At the time, my friend and I taught next door to one another. Every day we would walk to class together and every day she would wonder out loud if Preston would be in attendance that day. She knew if he was that her lesson plans would probably be useless.

So, what did she do? Read on.

Professional Boundaries: There Is a Fine Line

We are not friends with our students.

We are not friends with our students.

We can be *friendly* with our students but we cannot be friends.

For a million and one reasons, giving too much information about yourself, your home life, or your past, younger life, to students, expressing too much over-the-top emotion, or speaking in a "too cool for school" way are all no-nos. We definitely don't want our students to call us by our first names (unless that is the culture of your school and accepted by all).

We don't want to confuse students about our role in their lives. We don't want them texting us, showing up at our homes, or otherwise thinking we're a buddy. I've seen many teachers fall into the trap of what I'll refer to as friendship-thinking with students. I'll admit, it can be a short-term but effective way for a teacher to make an easy connection with students, but it's a trap. It makes it far too easy for a teacher to cross a line without really noticing. When this friendship-thinking happens, a teacher will speak too familiarly with students, which gives a green light to students to speak to that teacher (and maybe all teachers) in the same way. If we model a certain behavior then students will think it's okay to act that way too. How do you course-correct someone who is just following your example and not be a hypocrite? "It's okay for me to do this but it's not okay for you to do it" is not effective in the classroom-management sphere. In fact, this kind of thing usually results in a lot of anger, pushback, and non-compliance.

If we model a certain behavior, then students will think it's okay to act that way too.

Think about any professional development or training you've attended where you're being told that it's vital to be dynamic and engaging with your students but you are, in fact, dying of boredom because you're being talked *at* by trainers who are not dynamic or engaging. The hypocrisy usually doesn't sit right with us.

When I was just starting out in teaching, I hadn't totally learned the lesson about friendship-thinking yet. I became close with a struggling student, helping him succeed in subjects he hadn't had a lot of success with in the past. We got along, his mom and I were on great terms, and I felt like I was doing such a good job because he chose me to be his caring adult at school.

For weeks, he begged me to play a particular capitalist-leaning board game with him at lunch because I'd bragged a few too many times that I was a champ. That I was unbeatable. Ha!

To him, this was a signal that I was challenging him to a game to prove who was the actual champ.

At the time, I remember thinking, *What harm could it cause? It's just a game.*

I got into the game as competitive as always, forgetting for a moment or two that I was at work and had an obligation to be a mature adult and a professional. In the heat of the moment, when I made an error in purchasing a property, the student blurted, "Nice move, loser!"

Except he didn't say loser, he said something homophobic which happened to be in heavier use back then as common slang but was no less inappropriate.

I was stunned silent. His mouth dropped open and his face went scarlet. His friend, who was also playing, smacked him on the arm and told him to shut up and have some respect.

I didn't know what to do.

I realized, in that moment, that I'd blurred the lines of teacher and student and had been friendship-thinking throughout my interactions with this student. What he said was not good. It needed addressing, but the situation we found ourselves in wasn't his fault. It was all on me. He'd slipped, bantering more as he would with a friend than with a teacher because I'd allowed him to think that we were friends.

I'd put myself in a terrible situation because now I felt I needed to use discipline and I risked breaking the trust I'd shared with this student.

That trust had been built on a flimsy foundation.

Luckily, instinct kicked in. I've never been one to avoid confrontation and talk about things that are uncomfortable. Using a calm voice, I leaned in to what the student had said and asked him how he thought it would make someone who identified as homosexual feel when he used that word in a derogatory way. We discussed the common use of homophobic slurs and how much they hurt because they were so negative and had heavy meaning for anyone who was persecuted for being "different". We talked about where the terms came from and the connotation they have and why we're working to remove statements and judgements like slurs from our daily interactions. It was a good conversation in the end, awkward as anything, but it definitely went better than I thought it would.

I didn't lecture him about student and teacher boundaries and how inappropriate it had been for him to say something like that to me. That wasn't the lesson he needed. It was the lesson I needed.

That situation was what teachers like to call an ah-ha or teachable moment. Both for my student and myself. It changed how I interacted with students going forward.

When our unions and our administrations tell us to maintain boundaries with students, this is what they mean. I'm not saying you can't play games with your students. Games and gaming are valuable tools for learning and community building, and they can be an excellent reward system. I am saying that it's better to be the organizer and supervisor than a player if there is any risk of a student misunderstanding the relationship. You're the adult, you need to set the tone and understand how gestures, body language, and too much information can be taken the wrong way by the students in your care.

Just the other day I heard a student say to a teacher, "Hey, get over here!" as a way of getting her to speak to him about work he needed to do. He pointed at her, then gestured to his desk. Come here, *now*, was the message.

This teacher obeyed the student's command.

You might think, Why in the world did that teacher go along with such a rude request?

The teacher had already established a relationship with that student (and probably the entire class) that it was okay to speak that way to her. The student had an understanding that if he talked to his teacher that way, with that tone, he'd get the response he wanted.

It's as easy as that to blur a line. This is exactly, among other reasons, why we can't be perceived as friends to our students. We need to establish boundaries so that no one is confused.

Establishing Boundaries

In our role *in loco parentis*, the adult in the room, responsible for student safety and security, we have to make sure that students understand that we see them, we hear them, we value and respect them; however, we also need them to understand that while we are humans too, and we have stories we can share that they'll find entertaining, we will also expect them to behave in appropriate ways in our shared space. We, too, will behave in appropriate ways in our shared space.

We must be explicit in how we convey our behavior expectations.

We must be explicit in how we convey our behavior expectations. We can't expect students to guess or rely on what we believe is "common sense". As teachers, we need to teach them what is appropriate etiquette for speaking to one another and to adults. These soft skills, appropriate communication, and behavior expectations are not necessarily things they learn elsewhere.

Even in a common space, like, say, the hallway, if a student makes a demand of me that has an inappropriate tone, I correct them with a clear expectation, then offer an alternative way to say the same thing. Then we practice together.

Student: "You need to print this for me."

Me: "I don't usually respond to demands like that. Can you try that request again using different words?" Or, "Do you think that's the best way to ask me for help?" Or: "Mmmm, that's probably not a great way to start a conversation. How about we start with good morning. How are you? Could you help me print something, please? Now you try." I do this quietly, privately, and with a smile that holds zero sarcasm or attitude, which is difficult for me to do at times.

Students who start with an abrasive tone have learned to make requests of me in a kinder way and usually don't need a second reminder.

I set a boundary. They learn how firm it is by the way I interact with them.

ALL THAT BEING SAID

If a wild card student walks into your life, you *must* "befriend" them.

I don't mean invite them out for a shopping spree or to hang at the skate park or call them "bruh". You won't be able to use most of the strategies I've just told you about either. You definitely can't get away with the above interaction or correcting a wild card's tone. They will simply keep walking, pretend you don't exist, and/or escalate the situation. They don't care if you have boundaries, not at first, not if they don't know and respect you.

The wild card student needs delicate handling, which means they need more from you overall. More attention. More friendliness. More compassion. More effort to get to know them while at the same time not being overwhelming or annoying.

You need to be cool. Collected. Chill. You need to let them know you're happy to see them and mean it — or at least fake it so well that they believe it.

You need to edge up to the boundary of friendship-thinking so that you can find common ground, be able to joke a little, so that the wild card and you are on good terms. They need to understand you will bend some rules for them but you're no pushover. If done right, meaning that there is an understanding that you are willing to make the deals because you like them, not because you're scared of them, but that there are limits to the deals you make, then in exchange, you will have their cooperation.

Most of the time.

Which is better than none of the time.

It won't be easy to navigate. Not at first. You'll make mistakes. You'll cross too close or travel right into the friendship-thinking boundary but you'll learn (I hope) and grow and develop a sixth sense for the wild card and what you need to do to get them onside.

For all students, but especially the wild cards, if they feel seen and heard then they also feel valued and respected. A student who feels valued and respected will not only engage with learning but will also participate in your vision. And you need the wild card to be onside with you because if they aren't, then you may lose the rest of the class too.

Also, let's be real, there are always going to be more students than teachers in any classroom.

They have the numbers.

We need the students onside to have a successful year.

So, what did my friend do about Preston?

We knew Preston was capable of determining what my friend's teaching day would be like. We knew he could harness the entire class to do his bidding if he chose to. His mood would set the tone of the room.

She could have been offended by his power. She could have been hard and rigid and unwilling to give up control. She could have *attempted* to lay down the law with a stern, unyielding approach.

Instead, she got to know Preston. She gave him class time to share his stories and, believe me, he had some good stories. She gave him space to be himself. She didn't chastise him for coming late or missing class. She talked to him about his absences and let him know that, when he came late, he disrupted whatever she was trying do and that there were natural consequences that came with missing the first part of a lesson like missing out on a story she told or an important message that was shared. She did this in a way that was friendly but firm. She knew she likely wouldn't change his absenteeism, which had been going on long before her class, but she did manage to get him coming to class on time eventually.

How? Her class was one he enjoyed and felt safe coming to.

She didn't harp on him about breaking established classroom/school rules that were usually non-negotiables like putting his phone away, instead she'd give him a choice.

"Preston, you know you're not supposed to be on your phone right now. How about you put the phone in this paper bag on my desk while I'm teaching and you can have it back when I'm done. Or you can head down to the office to chat with Mr. Vice-P about your phone habits. I can call and let him know to expect you."

He usually defaulted to option one because he didn't want to miss out on what was going on in class, but sometimes he really did want to have a conversation with Mr. Vice-P and since he had a good relationship with the Vice-P, this was a consequence, yes, but not a heavy one.

On any given day, Preston set the tone for the class and the rest of the students would follow, so it was vital for my friend to get him onside with her.

She did that, very deliberately, by learning how to work with Preston's personality.

She allowed lessons to be derailed at times. She let Preston know that she valued his presence in her class and appreciated his personality. She also gave him, and the rest of the class, firm expectations about their success. She would do whatever she could to ensure they were achieving the goals they set out. She gave them time in class to work on things instead of assigning homework that she knew wouldn't get done. She extended deadlines as often as she could. She gave them extra chances to accomplish things. She had no secrets about how to do well. She gave feedback and shared tips openly and her students saw immediate results, which boosted their self-esteem and let them know that she could be trusted to help them succeed.

Preston liked his teacher. He liked the classroom. His teacher treated him firmly but fairly and she was consistent. He knew what to expect every day that he showed up.

Because he liked her, and as a bonus to getting the wild card onside, Preston would get the other students in line if they were fooling around or not listening while the teacher was teaching. He would keep them in line so she had fewer classroom management issues in general. This was especially helpful to my friend, because she had a reputation for being great with wild cards, so she had a class roster that was stacked with students who were notoriously difficult to manage.

With the wild card onside, things worked beautifully. Most of the time.

That is the power of the wild card.

And *that*, my friends, is pure gold.

Friendship-Thinking: The Fine Print

All that being said, please understand that even if you follow every piece of advice I give you, you won't reach every student. There will be a few over your long career whose armor you can't crack. There are reasons, beyond your skills and your compassion, that this happens sometimes. It might only be because you don't have enough time with that person or that their trauma is too deep for you to help in the time you have with them. You'll need to learn to accept that sometimes it's beyond your control and hope that somewhere in that student's life, at some point, they'll meet someone who does get through and whom they learn to trust. Also know that sometimes you can't reach a student simply because you're their teacher and no amount of trust building will make them see you as anything but the person forcing them to do something they don't want to do.

I will tell you, though, that some of those students who slip through the cracks end up building a relationship with you when you're no longer their teacher. I had a student who was a giant pain in the butt when I taught him. It was very clear that no matter what I did, I would never earn his respect. He was mouthy and argumentative. He scoffed at my lesson plans. He watched movies on his computer when he was supposed to be working. He walked out of class when he wanted and gave no apology when he came back. Calls to his home did nothing. Consequences were meaningless to him. When our time together ended, I wasn't exactly tearful to see him move on.

Two years later, I happened to be working with my class in the library when he came in. He accused me of nearly failing him when I taught him and I told him flat out, but kindly, that he was remembering incorrectly and should check his report card. I thought that was the end of the conversation. He'd merely come to stir me up as he loved to do.

As it turned out, he left and actually checked his report card. Then he came back and apologized for accusing me of something I didn't do. It was a humbling moment, and my perception of that student changed. From that point on we started talking. Every day, he'd stop by my classroom to chat. He'd shake my hand. We'd talk about his future plans. We'd talk about his current projects and homework. We'd talk a lot and, even though I hadn't built a satisfying relationship with him when I was teaching him, these informal check-ins led to a strong relationship after the fact.

It doesn't matter where you're situated, you need to always be ready to build relationships with students.

It doesn't matter where you're situated, you need to always be ready to build relationships with students. Even if you've had a negative experience with a particular student in one place, in a certain context, you need to be flexible enough to wipe that impression clean to make room for a new type of relationship to build.

It's really about you and whether or not you can be humble, set aside judgement and ego, and allow a relationship to form even if you know it'll take hard work.

Which leads us to the next power player.

In Short

- The most important thing you can do in this profession is make a priority of getting to know your students. Above curriculum, lesson plans, assignments, or homework, getting to know your students is the most powerful way you can pre-emptively derail classroom-management problems.
- There are types of students and patterns of behavior in schools and classrooms that can add a certain level of predictability to a classroom (or anywhere for that matter). Knowing that these patterns of behavior exist can prepare you for what you may find in a cohort.
- There also exists a wild card type of student who can change the dynamic of your plans and the essence or vibe of a room. You must get the wild card onside.
- We are not friends with our students but we should work at being friendly with them.
- We want to establish professional boundaries so we don't fall into friendship-thinking with our students. This means helping them understand where the line is that they can't cross by not crossing it ourselves.
- Relationships don't always develop while we're with a student in the classroom. Be open to developing relationships in the hallways, library, cafeteria. Even if you've had difficult experiences with a particular student, be flexible and open to working on a relationship in a different setting. You may be surprised by how different they can be.

Power Player Three: Is You!

I've heard many teachers say that students need to respect their teachers and in turn earn their teachers' respect.

This is what I like to call a logical fallacy.

It's not logical to demand respect simply because we're adult, educated, the teacher, or whatever label we decide automatically earns us respect, especially from someone who doesn't know us. We make the assumption that because we're "in charge" we automatically deserve reverence. That may have been the case in the past, when fear dominated the classroom with threats of corporal punishment, like rulers across the knuckles or a paddle to the rear end, but we've abandoned those practices because they're inhumane and outright abusive. Fear doesn't build community, at least not in a way that strengthens student self-esteem.

We can't stomp our feet and demand respect.

We need to earn students' respect.

We need to *earn* students' respect in order to be successful at our jobs. They don't owe us anything and, as the adults in the room, with, presumably, more life experience, we owe them an education that includes learning about empathy and compassion. Which we must model.

What's that old saying? Practice what you preach? Do that.

If it helps you to view this in a more "customer service" way, then you need to see your students as clients. We are in service to them and our goal is to ensure their success by teaching them how to be successful.

It reflects on us, in one way or another, if they don't succeed.

With respect comes trust and with trust comes engagement.

What this means, to put it bluntly, is that if you don't like children and/or adolescents, if you don't find some joy in spending a lot of time around students, if you simply can't be kind to a younger human being, you really shouldn't be in this profession.

Teaching is an incredibly important job. To me, it aligns in significance to any highly skilled profession that impacts a person's life. We, I believe, fall into the sphere of caregiver, no matter the age of our students.

The future of each student we interact with is in our hands. Their health and well-being and their success are dependent on how we engage with them.

If you think I'm exaggerating, do a quick internet search for studies on education and longevity or life expectancy. You'll be amazed at the findings. What you do. How you do it. It's actually a life or death thing.Your words and actions impact students. Every negative thing that happens is a barb that stays hooked into their psyches. They carry those traumas, even small ones, with them for the rest of their lives. The negative experiences tend to stick deeper and longer than any positive ones.

Strategy: Test Yourself

Try it yourself. Ask your friends and/or family if they remember something an educator said or did to them that made them feel big emotions. I bet they all have at least one story that they've carried with them that's negative.

I'll tell you mine.

My grade 1 teacher used to call me Red. Doesn't seem like much, does it? I have red hair. It was common in the '80s to call people with red hair "Red" as a nickname. Common in so much as two percent of the world population can be, that is. Obviously, Red isn't my name and when I was young I was extremely self-conscious about my hair because it made me stand out and I desperately wanted to fit in. I was shy and hated attention but because my fiery hair was different, I was often called Carrot Top or Soul-Eater, Ginger or Annie (you know, from that horrid musical). Some people even sang the infamous Annie song to me, "The sun'll come out tomorrow…" *Shudder*.

I loathed that movie and cursed its maker.

It gets worse. Not only was I teased with words, I would often get chased on the playground because of my red hair. I was the "It" of most games and usually the person last to be picked for teams because I looked "odd". Being different was not an asset. Another student even bit my back (yeah, I had to get a tetanus shot) because she wanted to taste my freckles. One memorable summer, I was attacked by a hummingbird that thought my hair was a flower! Okay, yes, that was cool but also, *come on*!

So imagine how it felt as a young, sensitive, quiet kid, to be nicknamed Red by my teacher. She was a brash woman who was both stern and a barrel of laughs (her laughs, our expense). Guess what happened next? My classmates started calling me Red too.

Do I think that teacher meant to traumatize me with the nickname? I hope not. She liked me. I was her "pet".

I truly don't think that my teacher was trying to hurt me. I believe she didn't reflect on or fully understand how much impact her words had on me.

She'd "outcasted" me. Marked me with a label that highlighted my difference. Her nickname gave the other students the green light to torment me. I was fair game to tease because I was different. I didn't even deserve to have a name other than the one my teacher had given me.

When I'd cried or worked up the nerve to complain about being bullied, I'd been called too sensitive and a tattle-tale.

There was no winning for me and no ally to turn to.

This is what one teacher's "harmless" actions can do to a student.

I can't tell you the number of times I've bumped into one of my former students in public, all grown up, who has shared stories with me about teachers who said things, even offhand comments, dismissals, or outright insults, that have stuck with them. Sometimes it motivates them to succeed when they were told they wouldn't ever succeed. They still have hurt in their eyes, even when they're telling me about the great things they've gone on to do.

It's my belief that our job *isn't* to motivate students to succeed out of spite. Or to prove us wrong. Our job is to help students see their potential and achieve their goals.

Our influence has power.

Our influence has power.

Be aware. Be mindful. Be intentional.

And above all else, do no harm.

Strategy: Welcoming Students

We must welcome everyone who enters our teaching space, genuinely, with positivity. Even on days that we're exhausted or have had a bad morning. Understand that children and teens are fragile in many ways, but their developing psyches are especially sensitive, so we need to make sure they know that we're happy to see them, we're concerned for their well-being, and they're welcome in our space.

For kindergarten, this needs to be done with acute consideration of the emotions coming into the space. It often takes younger kids more time to adjust to being away from home and getting used to a new space. Feeling alone and terrified is common. Starting with a calm, kind, and gentle approach each day can bring a sense of peace that helps ease some of that anxiety.

In general:

I wouldn't say, "Hey, Aiden. Happy Monday. You owe me an assignment."

I would say, "Hey, Aiden! Happy Monday. Did you have a good weekend? How was the amusement park?"

Business matters can come later, after we're settled in. My priority is to be welcoming, not demanding.

I wouldn't say, "Oh no! Abdul, are you crying again? What happened this time?"

I would say, "I'm sorry you're upset, Abdul. Do you want to tell me what happened or would you like to sit in the quiet corner and color for a bit?"

My goal with greeting students is to make sure they know that I care about their existence. Period.

Strategy: Top Priority — Know Names

Classroom teachers must absolutely know their students' names and use them appropriately, meaning: know their proper pronunciations and preferred names (and pronouns).

I typically give myself the first week of classes to memorize the names of my students. This might be easier or harder for you depending on your teaching assignment. Prep coverage teachers will have an obscene number of names to get right. Secondary teachers will likely have around ninety students with some repeats depending on what subject they teach. Elementary classroom teachers will have their class, with many students they may already know from previous years. I can, by this point in my career, memorize student names in about three days and be able to identify students by first name in the halls and outside the building.

Strategy: Learning Names

- Day 1: I ask students to make desk signs with their preferred names and pronouns by folding a piece of paper in three and creating a tent. You can use any kind of paper, as long as it's foldable, and pen, marker, or pencil, will show up on it clearly. You can even make this an activity for students to decorate their name tent with something about themselves.

- I ask students not to change seats (for older grades) at the start of the class every day for the first week. (*Note: I loathe seating plans mainly because I feel humans should be free to choose where they sit in any space. Giving students control over seating can sideline some behavioral issues by reducing students' anxiety about who they're sitting next to. That being said, not having a seating plan can also enhance certain behavioral issues.)

Note: I really like to see how students seat themselves and use it as a way of getting to know them. Whom do they sit with? Where do they seat themselves? Close to the front? Near the back? I only use seating plans if students are having difficulty following classroom guidelines or meeting expectations. I'm upfront with students about my seating plan feelings from the get-go where age-appropriate so they know that if I pull out a seating plan I'm not satisfied with how things are going.

Note: If I need to group students for a specific activity, I'm usually strategic about how I group them. If certain friends aren't the best working partners, I don't group them together. Otherwise, I let them choose groups, at least for the first few times. I learn a lot about students when I allow them to govern themselves. I always remind them that I hold veto power if a group isn't getting work done so they should choose their groups accordingly.

- In the first few days, while students are working on get-to-know-you activities and preliminary tasks, I move around the room (I always max out my steps in a day), chatting with students, noting their names, noting something unique to them. I usually set the seating/desk arrangements into groups of four/six, so I can bundle names together.

Note: Rows of desks may be needed, temporarily, if students are really having trouble following classroom guidelines, but I use them sparingly. Rows give a very "old school" vibe and tend to stifle participation and kill community even though they appear to enhance engagement because students are suddenly very attentive. At least for a little while.

- Also in the first few days, if a student moves for an activity, they take their name tent with them. In fact, I use the name tents in get-to-know-you activities as ways of introducing students to other students (more on this later).
- I collect the name tags at the end of each class, first in the order that the students are sitting, then I work towards mixing them up as I'm collecting them. At the beginning of each class, I test myself by matching the name with the student.
- If I make a mistake, I apologize, make a joke about my memory, then try again.

If you think knowing names isn't a big deal, think again. Names are powerful. They're meaningful. They can be loathed, loved, self-chosen, and gifted. Sometimes they hold trauma as well. I'm not a big fan of "name games" as get-to-know-you activities because I've witnessed them go awry in devastating ways.

I was once part of "sharing circle" in a classroom that I was observing and the teacher was doing an intro activity where each student shared their name and what it meant. As we moved around the circle, I noticed one student fidgeting quite a bit, not looking as excited or as unbothered as the other students. I assumed that she might be uncomfortable with speaking publicly and expected her to opt out of the activity. When it came time for this student to share, she squared her shoulders, took a step into the circle then broke into heart-wrenching sobs while explaining that she was named after her auntie who had been killed by a bomb in her home country.

Putting students in a situation that may not *seem* high stakes because, on the surface, sharing one's name seems like an easy entry point to community building can work against you and your good intentions. Be wary of activities that may ask too much of a student and try to think about the possible connotations that your activity may have. I once had a student tell me that he hated the "What's in your backpack?" get-to-know-you activity because when he was fleeing from his country he only had a backpack and in it were possessions he needed rather than ones he cherished.

We want students to get to know one another. It's vital for the community building of your room and the entire school.

We want students to get to know one another. It's vital for the community building of your room and the entire school, but we want to lower the stakes. Sharing one's name can be done in a more private way, with partners, small groups, as a more natural thing when starting an activity. "Introduce yourself to your group members or to your partner." It's not vital for everyone to understand the meaning behind one's name in order to get to know one another.

And if you absolutely *must* use an activity to dig into someone's name (keeping my story above in mind and the potential triggers you may hit) then I would give a lot of choice as to what and how students share.

Strategy: Interview Activity

Interview activities in partnerships could look like this:

- Each partner will ask: What is your preferred name? How do you pronounce it?
- Then each partner will answer one to three of any of the following questions:
  - Does your name have special meaning?
  - Why did you get your name?

Is there a story about your name?
Why do you like your name?
Why don't you like your name?
Does anyone else in your family share your name?
What were you almost named?
If you could change your name, what would you name yourself?
If you could pick a symbol for a name, what would you pick? Why?
What is your favorite name of a character in a movie/book/game? Why?
If you have pets, what are their names? How did they get those names?
What is the name of your favorite place to go? What is the name of somewhere you'd like to go?

Quick Tip: AI-generated questions can really help you come up with a lot of options. Of course, you need to review the questions carefully, with your class in mind, before putting the questions in front of students. If you're short on time and really committed to "name games" then use the tools available and give AI some directions to generate a list for you. Giving choice may help avoid triggering any student.

Getting to Know Your Students

It's not enough to know your students' names. You need to be able to talk to them about everyday things. If you know, for example, that Katie had a hockey game the night before, ask her how it went. If Aman was going to the dentist on the weekend and was nervous, check in, see how it went. Initiating little conversations like these takes no more than a few seconds but has a lot of value in relationship building. Not only does it tell your students that you genuinely care about what goes on in their lives, it also humanizes you in their eyes, especially when you validate them in some way. "Oh yes, cavities are the worst! I had to get three filled last year but the dentist made sure I didn't feel any pain at all." Or, "No cavities? That's awesome, Aman!"

There are a couple of things you need to understand about conversations with students. We are not social workers or therapists, so be cautious with life advice you're giving and with how you react to things.

For example, recently a student disclosed to me that she was sexually assaulted. I told her how sorry I was to hear that had happened to her. I was humbled that she felt comfortable telling me and tried to stay calm for her. Inside I was reeling, so upset that this had happened to her and disturbed by the details she had shared. I couldn't break down or flip out. I needed to stay as calm as possible so that she knew I was the right person to share her story with and that she could rely on me. We talked about next steps, and then together we went to talk to the principal so that the police and appropriate child services could be called.

Your students need to know, upfront, that you can't keep secrets that impact their well-being or the well-being of others. You have a duty to disclose/report and you need to explain that to students and remind them frequently. And if, like my student, they disclose something that upsets you, please do your best to keep your reaction calm and steady. They are sharing with you because they trust you and you need to model calm so that they stay calm. I know this can be a very big ask — we are human after all. You can freak out later when you have time alone, but try not to amp up an already stressful situation with an over-the-top reaction. Also, make sure you take care of your own well-being after a situation that causes you emotional stress. Your well-being is just as important as your students' and we all, at times, need care, repair, and nurturing to be the best we can be for our students.

How to Know Your Students

Students do not owe you information about themselves just because you asked them to share.

While getting information about your students is beneficial for building community in your classroom and helps you know your students better, it's important to remember that your students don't owe you anything. This means that if they don't want to disclose information to you, even if it's something that you think is benign, like hobbies, they are not obligated to share that with you. What might seem like harmless information gathering to you might be painful for a student. What if their favorite thing to do was knitting with grandma and she passed away over the summer? You don't know what's going on in a student's life, so keep the probing to a minimum. If a student isn't sharing, then they need more care and patience to build their trust.

As a matter of fact, if a student is not doing something (anything that is expected: activities, classwork, homework), it's a clue that there's something more going on. It could be something as simple as being unmotivated by that particular activity. Maybe they've done it one too many times and are over it.

Usually, people like to talk about themselves, so if a student isn't sharing then there's a reason for that. They might be shy to talk to other people. If a student isn't participating in an activity, they may feel self-conscious about what you're asking them to do. They may have cultural norms that don't fit with the activity you've planned. Or they may have done this activity in a different class and had negative results.

If you're able to find out the reason, whatever the reason, it's a valid reason, whether you agree with it or not. Do not push. Pushing a student will always create distrust when done without the student's consent.

There are ways to move a student forward so that they grow toward goals but forcing a student to share something they don't want to share is not the way to do it.

More on that later.

Strategy: Get-to-Know-You Activities

The first thing I'm going to say about get-to-know-you activities is that you really, really need to give students choice. I try to give at least three choices of activities and a variety of methods to deliver information. If you include choice, you'll find you'll have higher engagement, especially if you have easy and varied entry and exit points that are low-risk.

For example, asking someone to share what their all-time favorite anything is as an entry question is low-risk. Asking a student what they dislike about school is higher-risk.

Giving the option to answer in writing, orally to a partner, or as a drawing/collage is lower-risk than forcing a student to stand up and share something in front of the whole class. Having options reduces anxiety. Reducing anxiety increases engagement because it allows for safe risk-taking.

Of course, this is going to depend on grade and age range. Some groups of students need fewer choices because too much is confusing and overwhelming. Use your judgement and gauge how the class is responding, then adjust accordingly.

Some Ways to Learn about Your Students

Surveys: Surveys are useful but avoid asking students to express feelings about things too soon. If you haven't built trust, you'll make them uncomfortable. (*Having students share surveys with student guardians can help when gathering a detailed picture of life at home as well.)

Some standard survey questions might be:

- What do you like to do in your free time?
- Do you have a part-time job? Tell me more.
- Are you involved in any sports? Tell me more.
- Do you enjoy reading? Watching movies? Binging TV shows? Why/why not?
- Do you like to be around a lot of people, fewer people, or no people?
- Do you like to work alone or in groups?
- Who would you pick to work with in a group project?

- Carousel activities, where students decide what get-to-know-you activity they want to do, work really well. You can build a collection of activities and set them up in stations, then let students meander to the ones that most appeal to them. This can be done online as well using a HyperDoc or multimedia text selection tool. (*If you're unfamiliar with HyperDocs and text selection tools, do a search for them — you'll find templates and samples all over the place that you can tailor to the needs of your current students.)
- Round Robin discussions: Use teacher-generated random questions at table groups. Each student takes a turn answering the same question or even a different one. Or each table group has a different set of questions to answer, then the whole class rotates the question sheets, or they all physically get up and move to the next set of questions. You could even do this at chart-paper stations around the room and let students roam.
  Here are a few sample subjects for discussion:
  - When you eat cereal, do you like more milk than cereal or more cereal than milk?
  - Do you like the feeling of cold air on your cheeks on a wintery day? Tell us why.
  - What random objects do you use to bookmark your books?
  - Do you have chores? What are they?
  - Do you like to dance? Where? When?
  - Do you wear socks to sleep? Why, or why not?
  - Are you more into messy spaces or clean spaces? Why?
  - Do you like to play games? Tell us about some.
  - What is your favorite treat to eat?
  - What meal do you love the most?
  - Do you like singing/humming to yourself? Where do you do this the most?
- Four Corners activities: Using photos or faces or signs reading *Agree/Disagree/Strongly agree/Strongly disagree* posted in each corner of the room, ask students to go to the appropriate corner to pick a statement/picture that best matches their response to a statement you share. Statements should be

light-hearted. Cats are better than dogs. The book is always better than the movie. Cake is a good breakfast food.

  - Photos shouldn't evoke trauma but can show different states of being. For example, you can ask students how much energy they have and let them pick a corner with a picture that represents their energy level at that moment. One photo might be a lazy cat sprawled out with its head up, suggesting, "I'm here, I'm listening, but I'm not ready to do a lot." Another might be a sloth that is still at the bottom of a big tree looking up. Or it could be a photo of a hummingbird, wings on hyper-speed. This is a quick way to gauge where students are at, and you learn something about them in that moment. Also, it gets them up and moving, which does get some energy flowing.

- Would You Rather? There are a variety of ways to play this game — a spectrum that ranges from light-hearted to more serious. Would you rather eat a tub of ice cream or a tub of potato chips? Would you rather pet a cat or a lizard? Would you rather have all the money in the world or all the friends in the world? Would you rather get a job that you love but doesn't pay well or a job that you hate but pays very well?
- Partner Up. Introduce yourself to one other person and answer one of the get-to-know-you questions above. Then, take your name tents and find another pair. Introduce your partner to the new-to-you pair. Now answer a different question from the list. Make sure everyone gets a turn. Thank your group, then break off to form another foursome. (I've also done a version of this that is silent — no words allowed — so students have to get creative with communication. This is only possible after students get to know each other and are comfortable; otherwise the silence is awkward, which is not what you want.)
  - If you're setting up groups for an activity, you can use get-to-know-you strategies like: All the people who love the color yellow, sit here. All the people who love purple, sit here.

Hint: Using activities that get students up and moving is a great way to amplify the energy in the room no matter the grade. Keep that in mind if you need to ramp down the energy in a classroom as well.

All of the activities I've used above can be put into lesson plans to teach concepts or reflect on learning as well. So introductory activities like these can act as scaffolding that gives opportunity for safe practice before getting into learning tasks and higher-stakes activities.

For example, if we've already used Four Corners to learn different likes and dislikes students have, then they're familiar with the activity so we can use Four Corners for reviewing different math problems/rules that students have been learning and gauge how well it's sticking.

The list above is nothing compared to the many, many activity ideas available to us on the internet. You can find just about any kind of activity with a little search engine sleuthing. Not only that, but AI also provides some very interesting suggestions when you ask it for activity ideas. Just make sure you're tweaking whatever you find to reflect the needs of the students in front of you.

When it comes to get-to-know-you activities, I not only give students options in what questions they answer and how they respond, I also include an opt-out choice. A pass or opt-out strategy is one I use as I'm building community because sometimes the stress of sharing is overwhelming for a student and my goal isn't to embarrass anyone or put them on the spot. My goal is to build a safe space. A student who opts out regularly is one I need to spend more time with to uncover why they prefer not to share. Once I figure out what keeps them quiet, I can then make accommodations so that they feel included rather than left out. Sometimes this means that they share their responses on paper and a friend reads it out loud. Sometimes we set a goal for the student to try and speak in class once a week. Sometimes we have a simultaneous online chat going on where quiet students contribute to the conversation in writing.

One size doesn't fit all, all the time.

I make sure the get-to-know-you activity suits the cohort I'm with. One size doesn't fit all, all the time. You might start with the same activity each time you meet students at the beginning of a school year or semester, but depending on what you learn about them you might find your usual repertoire isn't going to work.

As with most things, you don't want to force it, especially when you're trying to build community.

What Do I Do while Students Are Getting to Know Each Other?

I take notes as I'm walking around the room, listening, participating here and there, but mostly observing and collecting information. I use the first month of class for heavy data gathering. I sometimes have a clipboard where I jot notes down or go back and forth to my computer to take information down (I set my laptop up in different places around the room each day so I'm not running back and forth to the teacher desk). I let my students know what I'm doing and if they ask to see my notes, I show them. I don't collect information to use against students, ever. This is a fact-finding mission so I can strengthen my relationship with students, not a gotcha strategy.

*A gotcha is a calculated trap which is used to shame students and/or penalize them, for instance by deducting marks. My recommendation is that you never use a gotcha, for any reason. It's cruel.

There is no place for judgements in any notes I take as I'm getting to know my students.

I'm not going to lie, this takes a tremendous amount of work up front. At the beginning of each year I spend most of my time getting to know my students, more time than I spend on teaching curriculum. I've learned that knowing my students is more valuable than anything else in terms of helping them achieve success and managing behavior. If I don't spend time on relationship building then nothing I do later will stick as well as it can. It's especially important for classroom management.

With classroom management, the more work you do upfront, the easier managing behavior will be later.

The more work you do upfront, the less you'll have to do later.

When students enter the classroom at the beginning of class, I welcome them, by name. Sometimes I stand at the door, holding it open for them and sometimes I walk the room as they come in and get settled. I've seen teachers do special handshakes or elaborate dances to welcome students in, which is entertaining to watch, but not really practical on a daily basis. No judgement if that's your thing and the students are into it. You do you.

Over the week I touch base with each student about something I know. "Is that the sweater you were telling me about? Looks fantastic!" "Did you go on a camping trip this weekend? Did you enjoy it?" "How's the puppy doing? Learning new tricks still?"

Be prepared to spend a minute or two with each student at some point every week, or every day if you happen to see them a lot. If you see your students for a limited time each day, try to connect as often as you can, even if it's in the hall or outside during recess or at lunch, before or after school.

One word of caution: When interacting with students in the hall, be prepared for the unexpected answer. Just last September, I asked a student I didn't know very well but had talked to a few times how his summer had been as I was on my way to the staffroom.

He replied, "Not that great, actually."

Still walking, now keeping pace with him, I asked, "Oh, that's not good. What made it not great?"

"Well, my mom died," he said.

My. Mom. Died.

I stopped walking. He stopped walking. This needed to be an actual conversation rather than a drive-by one.

His mom had been sick for a long time, battling cancer. He told me all about it. Shared his feelings. Hit me with it all.

I told him how sorry I was, then asked if he wanted to connect with one of the admin or talk to our school's social worker. He told me that he'd rather just go play soccer outside.

As we parted, I beelined to the office to make sure everyone who needed to know knew. I wanted to make sure the student had support if he needed it.

An innocent question, meant to start a quick chat, turned into something much more impactful. Be prepared for anything when you ask a student something about themselves.

Strategy: Test Yourself

How do you know if you're winning at knowing your students?

- Get a piece of paper or open a blank document.
- Jot down the names of your students in the order you remember them (first name is fine; last name too = expert level).
- Miss anyone? That's who you need to spend more time with. Who was first on your list? Why? Who was last? Why? Do some reflecting on how you spend your time with your students and where you might shift for maximum relationship building.

I use this activity, and variations of it, throughout the time I'm with a particular class. For a little extra challenge, I'll test myself on things I know about each student as well. You can find a lot of different versions of this kind of activity online with a simple search. Find one that works for you and use it at least once a term. I've included a template for you to consider. It's a really easy way to see how well you're connecting with your students.

Template: Test Yourself

Student Name (First)	**Bonus! Student Name** (Last)	**Student Fact(s) — My Guess** (e.g., Hobby, Pet, Favorite Subject)	**Actual Fact/ Detail(s)_** (Confirmed Information)	**Notes/Next Step**
Example: Allison (Allie) She/Her	*Dupuis*	*Loves dogs* *Likes to read* *Plays soccer*	*Has a husky named Chance* *Reads romance and fantasy* *Has soccer practice on Tuesday afternoons and games usually on the weekends*	*Provide alternate due dates and timelines to accommodate soccer schedule. Find more romance/fantasy for class library.*

Pembroke Publishers ©2026 *How to Win at Classroom Management in 6 Easy Steps* by Angie Barrett ISBN 978-1-55138-375-0

Tenets to Live By

Be nice. *Especially if you're annoyed.*

- If a student has been away, let them know you're happy to see them (this is especially important for wild card students). As much as you might want to throw a little sarcasm at them — "Thanks for finally joining us, Isla!" — shaming a student won't build trust. In fact, it usually will cause someone to want to spend *less* time in your class.
- Seeing students doing something they shouldn't be doing (I'm not talking about dangerous things here) should be met with curiosity before anger.

For example, if I'm on hall duty and there are way too many students milling about, out of class, I approach casually, smiling or at least not frowning, with a relaxed posture and open expression. This means that my arms aren't crossed, I'm not marching toward the students, and my voice is steady and calm.

If I know one of them, I use their name. Otherwise, I say, "What's everyone up to today?" or "How's your day been so far?" or "What has your attention here?"

Listen, and I truly mean *listen*, to their answers. Don't interrupt. Don't have a snappy comment locked and loaded. Be interested.

"That sounds wonderful and I'm glad you've been able to connect with your friends. The bell went a while ago though, so let's move things along." Sometimes I offer to escort students to their class.

If there's an obvious problem then I use the same calm approach but ask, "How can I help?" or "What can I do to help fix this?" or "Is this the best decision right now?"

The younger the student, the less independence they usually have, the more investigating you need to do.

The younger the student, the less independence they usually have, the more investigating you need to do.

Interactions with students should be courteous at all times, even if you're on hall/yard duty and spot a group of students who are notorious for being troublesome. Even if you've had a negative experience with some of them. Even if you don't know them at all but you *do* know that they're somewhere they shouldn't be.

Courteous doesn't mean you can't be firm. Remind students what the expectations are, just in case they don't know, "We always clean up after we eat in here." "Let's not leave a mess for someone else to clean up." Then follow with a direct, calmly stated directive. This works just as well on five-year-olds as it does on eighteen-year-olds. "Before you leave, I need you to put your garbage in the trash, okay? Thank you."

No one would ever say that I'm a push-over with students. Flexible, yes, but also firm.

Here are some other tenets I practice in classrooms:

- Avoid threats, attacks, and gotchas. We don't want to humiliate or trap our students. Fear and shame are not motivators.
- Suspend judgement as much as possible. As social humans, I realize that judgement is part of how we function; however, I do try my best to keep an open mind when I'm interacting with students. It doesn't always work and sometimes I unfairly judge a situation or a student. When that happens, I apologize and strive to do better, then work hard to earn back the trust I broke.
- Monitor your tone of voice: I'm a liberal user of sarcasm but sarcasm against a student isn't good, *ever*. You can joke using sarcasm *with* a student but never at the expense of a student. Even if you don't think you're being

mean, you might hit a sensitive spot that ruins a person's day/month/entire school year.

- Listen to the person who is talking. Put your phone down, look away from your computer, whatever it is you are doing, stop and hear what your student has to say. If you can't do that, then ask them to pause for a few minutes until you can. I find it so odd when a teacher who has solid rules about paying attention in class fails to do so when talking to a student. If you can't abide by your own expectations then why would students?
- Avoid interrupting or talking over a student. It's rude in general and tells a student that what they have to say has no merit as far as you're concerned.
- Check your facial expressions: my face tells it all so I really have to work at being genuine with my words because my face is going to broadcast the truth.
- Eye contact is important but not always. Remember that sometimes eye contact is offensive and prolonged eye contact can turn into a stare-down that leads to escalation.
- You should never be the reason something escalates. Your goal is to deescalate by looking for ways to calm the situation down rather than amp it up.
  - Sometimes that means giving in to something a student wants and feels is worth fighting for. Sometimes it's making an exception, one time, for extenuating circumstances. Sometimes offering choice is the way to go. "Elijah, I understand you're done your work and that's awesome but I'm not okay with you interrupting your friends while they're working. You can go and sit quietly in the book nook and read or you can sit quietly at your desk and color." Try to offer things that will normally appeal to the student. If you offer them something you know they hate, you're going to escalate the situation.
  - Sometimes, escalation is unavoidable because a student isn't going to back down or take an "out" you offer them. In those cases, calling an end to the conversation is the best path. First validate their feelings, "I understand you're upset, or I think we both might be upset." Then, "Let's talk about this in ten minutes." Or, "Let's take a break and talk later."
    (* Know your limitations. At times, you may need to seek help from support staff, Special Ed/Student Services teachers, and/or administration because the student is struggling with something that they can't manage their emotions over and it's beyond your realm of influence or expertise.)

I once had a student who would fight me on every grade he earned. He'd storm my desk and demand, in front of the class, to know why he got the grade he did. He'd be furious, spitting mad. Even though I would try to deescalate the situation, he wouldn't have it.

The entire class knew why he earned the grades he did. He was always clowning around. Never listening. Making jokes while I was teaching. Didn't do the practice activities and made sure everyone knew he wasn't doing them. He wouldn't accept offers of help and handed in most things hastily done and late. So his very authentic, angry outbursts when he saw the results were met with the baffled looks of some students and the full-out belly laughs of others.

It was the worst class experience I've ever had. I actually stopped teaching that grade for years afterword because I felt so traumatized. It didn't seem to matter what I did; I couldn't get through to this student. Even trying to sit with him to go over assignments and rubrics wouldn't help. He was always escalated by that point and I wasn't skilled enough at classroom management to realize that I needed to stop him from escalating in the first place. Sure, I would try to give him feedback and get him to work with me before due dates but he wouldn't do it. I reached out to his parents but that resulted in more anger from him. His outbursts were so over-the-top that I dreaded handing his assignments back.

I didn't understand at the time, but I later learned that he was being relentlessly bullied and hazed by his hockey team. His self-esteem was in the gutter and his bravado in class was so huge that nobody knew just how bad things were for him. Did that impact how he behaved with me? Maybe. I think there was a lot going on for him. I was seeing the tip of the iceberg. He had so much ambition and not enough patience. Maybe there was a diagnosis missing there somewhere. Whatever the case, he was going through something and I was ignorant of it.

I know I did my best with what skills I had at the time. He was a wild card, for sure, and I'd managed to bond with him enough that he'd wanted a group picture with me and his class buddies to remember what a great time he'd had in my class that year. *Um... What?* He enjoyed my class? We had very different experiences, I guess.

I still have the picture. I don't look at it often.

I do wonder if, knowing what I know now, I could have done something different to help him deal with what he was going through, or perhaps alert someone who could help him more than I could. I didn't know what was going on but maybe I could have if I'd set aside my frustration and really got to know him, earn his trust more, show more compassion and care. Maybe I could have been more empathetic. Maybe I could have been sterner with stronger boundaries.

My point is that sometimes we just don't get through in the way we would like to. We can't save all our kids, and that's one of the brutal facts of teaching life.

Classroom Tenets Continued

- Use non-judgemental statements that convey empathy and/or validate feelings: "I understand how this must feel." "I realize this is hard." "I understand why you're upset."
  - Encourage self-validation: "I have a right to be angry." "What you said really made me mad." And your response to this is to listen and avoid saying, "Yes, you do, but you shouldn't act that way here." Try instead, "Yes, you're right, it makes sense that you're angry and I'd like to figure out how to fix this."
- Use a non-threatening approach in your interactions, even serious ones. You might not approve of a student's behavior but you can tolerate it (as long as it isn't dangerous) while you get to the bottom of what is causing it to happen.
  - For example, I once had a student who sought attention, mostly negative attention, with over-the-top displays of defiance. I had hall duty one day and when he caught sight of me, he hopped onto a table and began shouting and acting like a carnival announcer. As I got closer and began telling him to get down, he amped up the show. Walking up and down the table, singing, being a real crowd pleaser. The table was sturdy by my assessment and I knew in that moment that there was nothing I could do to get him down short of catching one of his arms and yanking him off the table, which I wasn't going to do. So I walked away. *No audience, no show.* I played it very cool but it was one of the hardest things I've

ever done in the realm of behavior management. It was so risky and I was stressed that he could fall. That he'd hurt himself. That he could hurt someone else or that another student might get on the table too. The reality was, even if I was watching, all of that could have happened.
    - Even though my back was turned, I was fully attuned to the noise and knew exactly when the show stopped. It didn't take long. Maybe a few seconds of him realizing that I was leaving. I didn't look back until I was about to round the corner and when I did, he was looking at me, frowning, and I knew then and there that we had a new understanding between us.
- Look for clues in the words and reactions you're seeing, and be aware of what might be under the surface of how a student is acting. For example, if a student is refusing to do something you've assigned, try to figure out if they don't understand the instructions or if they had a bad morning at home and are out of sorts. Maybe they're hungry, tired, or have had an argument with a friend and can't focus. All of these things, and more, can contribute to what you see as disruptive behavior.
- Smile. Not in a creepy way but naturally if you can. If smiling doesn't come naturally to you, try to take the customer service approach to your interactions. Being pleasant, helpful, and friendly goes a lot further than any other means of interacting with someone.
- Keep in mind that you've probably had a lot more experience in life than your students. Students at any age, any grade, simply haven't had the same number of years to accumulate education, life events, and training as most teachers, so holding them to "common sense" standards that might be easy for a professional grown-up can be more difficult for students. Especially when they haven't been explicitly taught. *Think about that the next time you give a multiple-choice test without teaching how to study for, then write, an MC test.
- As a general rule, try not to be dismissive, even if it's something like telling a student everything will be fine. You don't have a crystal ball. You probably can't tell the future. Encouraging a student to look at the positive side of things can come across as dismissing their legitimate concerns. Respond with empathy and sincerity: "That sounds awful." "That must have been so stressful." "What do you need right now?" Offer a quiet place. A walk around the school. A trip to the library. A snack. A listening ear. Sometimes all a person needs is someone to vent to.
- You definitely want to be inclusive, calling in rather than being exclusive and calling out even when you're dealing with serious and uncomfortable topics. Remember, shaming someone isn't the best way to help them learn anything. We want students to grow with learning, not shrink. So if something happens that treads into racism, for example, rather than reacting with anger or a chastising tone, start with curiosity. Ask why a statement was made that way, where it came from. Probe into what the student/all students know. Correct with kindness and understanding and stress the importance of not hurting one another with hateful language and ideas. Also be firm. Hurting someone isn't negotiable. It's a teaching moment. Use it. Nobody learns better ways of being human if they're being yelled at or shamed.
- If your lesson plan goes off the rails and something you've planned has an unintended consequence or doesn't work the way you envisioned, you need

to be upfront about the mistake, then, when everyone is ready, move to something different. For example, say you planned a Health lesson where students will create mini-skits in order to teach one another about healthy eating habits. Some students, trying to be funny, began planning jokes in their skits that called others out. Other students felt too shy to plan a skit. Others only wanted to do the skit privately with no audience. You realize that, while the information is important, the activity you planned is too high-risk. In order to deescalate the energy, you let the students know that the activity isn't working the way you thought it would so you're going to park it for now.

- Change activities to something less threatening (coloring, watching a funny video). Sometimes you can pivot to a conversation about what went wrong and how to improve (this will depend on age/grade and how grievous the mistake was). Sometimes a reset can be something as simple as turning the lights out for some decompression time.

I'll admit, the first step toward winning at classroom management is more like a giant leap. I've covered a lot, I know. And you might be wondering why I've spent so much time on set-up and understanding the power players. When it comes to classroom management, prevention is always the first step to success and, in order to prevent issues, you need to do the most you can to anticipate where issues might crop up. This is done through careful consideration and planning.

If you waltz into a space expecting students to be sitting quietly waiting for you to share wisdom, then you're in for a shock. You have to be prepared, especially when you don't have a lot of successful experience to pull from. If you spend the time upfront, you'll set your students up for success, which means you'll set yourself up for success as well.

In Short

- Respect is a two-way street in our profession. We need to earn student respect and give students respect, unconditionally. We must model the behavior we expect from students.
- This profession isn't going to be right for you if you dislike children and/or adolescents. If you can't tolerate spending time with students, you probably should consider a different job.
- Teaching is an incredibly important, skillful job. Because we impact people's lives in significant ways, we need to have the mindset of someone who genuinely cares about students' well-being, sees their potential, and wants to help them reach their goals. We must make sure they believe that we are happy to see them and welcome them into the learning space.
- Learn your students' preferred names and pronouns with proper pronunciation. Give yourself a short timespan to get it right. It's incredibly impactful when you know how to acknowledge your students properly.
- Get to know things about your students with the understanding that they don't owe you information about themselves. You can't force them to share but if they do, use the information you get to help build a stronger relationship with them.
- Give students choice when using get-to-know-you activities. Choice allows for easy entry and safe risk-taking. Include an opt-out strategy.

STEP 2

Share Expectations and Stick to Them

I have never met a student who is a mind reader. Yet students are often expected to be able to reach into a teacher's mind and pull out what they're thinking.

Expecting students to simply "know" the rules of the classroom space suggests that they are indeed mind readers. You might argue, "But they've been in school for X number of years! They should know by now!" Or my favorite, "It's common sense!"

I'm here to tell you that it's not common sense and it's not fair for anyone to be judged and, often, punished for something that they may never have been taught to do or not to do.

It's your *job* to:

- Set Expectations.
- Teach What They Mean.
- Model the Expected Behavior.

Be Fair but Firm

Setting expectations can be done in a variety of ways.

- You may be the type of teacher who likes things "old school" and take inspiration for classroom rules from a more traditional stance.
    - Students will raise their hand and wait to be called on before they speak.
    - Students will remain in their seats for the entire class time.
    - Students will be silent at all times unless asked to speak.
    - Students will show respect to the teacher and their classmates.
    - Students will ask for permission to leave the room.

  Very controlled. You are in charge. Good luck with that.
- You may be the type of teacher who wants students to co-create class guidelines. Co-creating with students is incredibly time-consuming but extremely valuable. It helps fast-track community building if done correctly and is a very diplomatic way of setting the rules, but again, it'll

take up a lot more time than you're expecting. The process goes something like this:

- Students brainstorm classroom rules they have experienced or heard about. This can be done in small groups, pairs, or independently. You can have students use sticky notes to put ideas on chart paper around the room to give a little more anonymity (which of course opens up the possibility of pranks/inappropriate suggestions). You can have students work in carousel stations where they brainstorm "what if" scenarios. What if a student has to leave the classroom? What should they do first? What if a student doesn't follow instructions? What happens to them? Etc. Use whatever means you want to gather information and suggestions from your students.
- Then sort the information into themes. This can be done as a whole-class activity, in partners, or in small groups or you can quickly do it yourself while students are generating ideas. For example, if you get a lot of ideas about how to participate in class and what happens if a student comes late to class, bundle those together so you have a starting place.
- In groups, or pairs, or in whole-class discussion, students will analyze the merits of the ideas in the themed chunks. You'll need to teach students how to analyze, for example, using the concept of pros and cons. They will need to learn how to debate respectfully and how to speak to one another in a way that effectively conveys points. This can be a great way to introduce aspects of effective discussion/debate/communication for a later unit, giving them time to practice and get comfortable with how to do it.
- I usually give students a short list of "look-fors" such as:
- This rule:
  - respects the rights of others/is fair;
  - doesn't disrupt what we're doing in the classroom;
  - doesn't hurt anyone;
  - doesn't break any of the school rules.
  - (*Add whatever you think students should consider when building classroom rules.)
- Students then vote on the "best of". (*Teacher has veto power to tweak where needed but this should really be done through feedback during the process. Teacher should be part of the process and add thoughts as each group is debating. Because this is a democratic process, we don't want to ruin it by being overly dictator-like and we absolutely don't want to do all this, then impose our own rules instead. Students do not appreciate having their time wasted.)
- Class guidelines/rules are established, then revisited after some time has passed to make sure they're still working for everyone.

• You may be the type of teacher who sets the expectations (possibly with student input) but does it in a way that is fair and flexible and appropriate for the age range.

  These are some of the expectations/guidelines I've used:

  - Two students at a time can leave the classroom for five minutes. Please get my attention before you go and write your name on the sign-out log with the time you leave. Sign back in when you come back. (*Students might like or need more flexibility in extenuating circumstances. I once had a student who suffered from colitis and needed to *go* when he needed to go, immediately. I'm not a monster, and there were no restrictions on him leaving the classroom. I did check in with him occasionally to make sure we were on the same page about my expectations. I expected him to leave and come back to class respectfully and not wander off or waste time. He never abused my trust, but if he had, disappearing for longer than necessary or getting distracted in some way, I would have followed up with him, then called home for reinforcement of my expectations.

- I ask for hands up during class discussion so that things don't get too chaotic. (*That's my general base rule, but if we're debating, I teach the students how to participate without hands so the conversation flows. If we're brainstorming, I teach them how to throw ideas out so I (or a student) can record them.)
- Eating is permitted during class time. I would never stop a student from eating. We need food to help our brains work.
- I don't want to see phones. Especially when I'm teaching. No earbuds/headphones in until it's time to work. Of course, this depends on the class and what accommodations may be needed. Some students require noise-cancelling headphones to help them focus.
- I have my non-negotiables: Don't touch anyone without consent. Don't bring peanut products into the classroom.
- My students can sit where they like. I advise them to choose wisely so they're not being distracted from their work and learning. (*I will use a seating plan as needed, depending on the cohort and the behavior. More on this shortly.)

No matter the method, it's your responsibility to teach students what the expectations mean. I start with finding out what they already know (meet them where they are), then go from there, but always explicitly explain the purpose and meaning behind a rule (yours, the school's, the board's). Yes, that means you can't just tell them, "That's the way it is so deal with it," or because "I'm the boss," or because "I said so."

Model what you want to see. Don't be glued to your phone if you don't want students on theirs.

Model the actions you wish to see in your students. If you don't want them on their phones, don't be on yours. If you want them to speak respectfully, make sure you do as well.

I've witnessed teachers speaking in an incredibly playful manner with students, throwing insults meant to be funny, but when a student throws one back, the teacher gets upset and escalates to anger or offense immediately. If you dish it out, you need to be prepared to take it. And I strongly suggest you not dish it out if you don't want classroom management issues later on. Being overly playful can be confusing to students and cross boundaries.

Whatever you want them to learn, you need to give them a model of what it looks like to be successful and give them time to practice without penalty.

General Tips for Sanity

- Establish routines. Students, no matter the age, love knowing what's coming next, day by day, week by week. It's a super-easy way to reduce anxiety for students about the unknown. You can't, obviously, prevent surprises from cropping up but having a routine will reduce the escalation of undesirable behavior when things don't go as planned. The point here is that students need to know what to expect each day or every other day, so they can settle that part of their brains that doesn't like surprises; it gives them a sense of security which goes a long way in regulating emotions — which means, it makes classroom management easier.

- Routines can be very regulated in terms of every minute of every day being accounted for, or a little loose so students know what they are expected to do for fifteen-to-twenty-minute chunks of time and those chunks might change from day to day.
- I'm a huge fan of chunking lessons with the idea that my voice isn't dominating for more than ten minutes for senior, five to seven minutes for intermediate, and two to three minutes for junior. You'll only have a person's attention for so long before they need to get moving or doing something. I'd much rather students drive their learning than be forced to listen to me lecture.
- Whatever the rules/guidelines are, whether they're co-constructed, teacher-created, or overall school protocols, be consistent in your approach and handling.
  - Don't tell students one thing but do another. For example, if there is no food allowed in a certain area, don't break that rule for anyone, not even yourself, unless you have a darn good reason that makes sense, like a special occasion. (*Being the "boss" of the room isn't a good enough reason, by the way.)
  - Don't change a non-negotiable rule willy-nilly day by day. That's super-confusing. Imagine you're driving and suddenly a stop sign means "Only stop if your car is green." Then blue. Then purple. Not fair or sensible.
  - Do bend rules that require flexibility. Maybe you let a student read quietly instead of doing math work because they're super-anxious and need a few minutes to settle their emotions. Wild cards need rule bending because they're going to push limits all the time and you won't be able to withstand the storm if you don't bend a little.
  - This one might be a little controversial, so proceed with caution:

- Break rules that are oppressive: for example, if the dress code doesn't sit right with you, maybe look the other way when a student isn't sporting a two-inch strap. A lot of dress codes are oppressive and were made without student input. I agree that there probably should be some guidelines around what to wear but it should perhaps be more about weather and comfort and less about traditional ideas that are oppressive. Maybe stand up for a student if they get harassed about it by someone else. Some rules uphold oppression and need to be obliterated. Choose your battles. (Schools requiring uniforms generally have stricter guidelines which must be obeyed by all.*)
  - If you decide to act punitively as discipline:
    - Do not tie it to grades. Please, for the love of cats, tying punishment to grades means you're ignoring the purpose of assessment and evaluation, which is to improve student learning ("Growing Success," 2010). Arbitrarily deducting marks for behavior means that you think grades are a measure of behavior. They are not. They're a measure of the learning that's happening or that has happened. More on this later.

- Do not loop in some kind of subject-specific punishment. I remember covering a class who were being held back from time in the gym for Phys Ed class (which they loved) due to misbehavior. Their task was to write an essay about what they did wrong the day before. Ouch. Yuck. Why encourage the unfair hatred toward essay writing by making it a punishment? How is essay writing connected to the behavior from the day before? Why is essay writing the punishment and not math equations? Afterward, the teacher tossed the essays out without reading them. In front of the students, no less! Talk about being disrespectful. Phys Ed has curriculum expectations, which means you definitely don't want to send the message that work for Phys Ed is a throwaway subject to be discarded. There are ways to keep the learning going without using an essay as a form of discipline. Maybe we cover a health lesson that day instead of using the gym. Maybe we go through expectations, revisit co-created rules for safe and appropriate gym use, and do an activity around that since students are struggling with their behavior.
- Don't use empty threats. If you've made a big deal about students getting a detention for some infraction, make sure you follow through. The fastest way to lose legitimacy in the eyes of your students is not following through. This is also true if you make a promise about a reward. Stick to your word.
- Do not use shame. I've dealt with this already but shame is such a powerful emotion and many students are hard on themselves and their self-esteem as it is. Don't add to the pain they already feel by shaming them over something at school. That means, no names on the board for missing work, no calling out for the whole class to hear, no using peers to put pressure on other students (talk about condoning bullying).
- Also mentioned before, do not use gotchas. This means, don't set your students up for failure just to teach them a lesson. I see this when I watch fails on social media. Oftentimes the fails are completely preventable but the person who is taking the video, obviously and seemingly without remorse, doesn't stop a "fail" from happening, even if they know someone will get hurt, because it makes for a good video. I think that's pretty terrible. Telling a student it's okay to break a rule as a test to see if they will, then punishing them if they do, is pretty terrible too, yet, I've seen it happen.
- Do not exclude students from something fun and community-based (sometimes this is done because of grades). I've seen withholding field trips used as punishment for a student who has misbehaved or is getting low grades. It is believed to be a motivator but no one else had to earn the trip and no rubric/checklist was given out stating the standards by which a student was being evaluated in order to come on the trip in the first place. Not only are you excluding someone from a group activity but you're denying them the learning that trip is meant for. Field trips are connected to the curriculum, right?
- Do not put hands (or any other body part) on a student. I wish I didn't have to say this, I truly do, but I've seen it happen in the heat of the moment, especially when a teacher is fed up and riled up. The only

people who can put hands on a student are the ones with special training to do so.
    - Do not ever confine a student. No locking them in a room. No taping their mouths shut. No tying them to a chair. Don't even joke about doing that. It's not funny.
- Offer choice in punishment — a menu of options. Make sure it's time-limited and specific to the rule that was broken. I mentioned how choice was used in my friend's class with the wild card but in general you want to give no more than three choices, all desired outcomes for you and not soul crushing for your student.

Proximity is king.

- Proximity is king. This is why I rarely sit at the teacher desk or stay in one place while I'm teaching. If a student is doing something distracting or on the forbidden list (like using a cell phone or fooling around), use proximity to quietly remind that student of the rules. If standing close by (not hovering) doesn't work, then I tap the student's desk lightly. If that doesn't work, then I quietly remind the student of the relevant rule and ask them to correct course. I then redirect the student to the task they should be working on.
- Remove emotion from your interaction. A calm steady voice goes a lot farther than yelling. Yelling makes you come across as unhinged and scary. We don't want our students to be scared of us if we're trying to build community in a classroom. You can be stern without being heated.
- Allow natural consequences. When I say this, I don't mean watch as a student sticks out their foot to trip another student and wait for the natural consequence of gravity to take over. I mean, sometimes a natural consequence of not using class time wisely means homework.
- High-stakes things (like grades) require another chance. Be compassionate whenever possible. If a student missed a deadline because they were fooling around instead of working in class, give them a second opportunity, with restrictions, to get something handed in. It's a great learning opportunity for them about not only compassion but time management. Make sure you contact home to let parents/guardians know about the second opportunity and your expectations.
- Be willing to negotiate and be open to alternatives. Giving students ownership over the consequences of their actions is as important as teaching them accountability. Students tend to default to pretty harsh punishments for themselves (remember when I said they already do a number on their self-esteem) so helping them reach more reasonable consequences is another learning opportunity.
- Don't overuse consequences. When I say this, detentions come to mind. So many detentions. I have never given one single detention in my career to date. Why? Because I consider it a punishment for me. I don't want to stay after school or at lunch/recess with a bunch of sullen students sitting quietly or writing lines or whatever it is teachers who give detentions make students do. I've noticed that teachers who overuse this punishment tend to have to spend many of their lunches in detention. I really can't fathom what learning is supposed to be happening when the same students end up in the same space every day. I wonder, too, if the same students put themselves in detention because they would rather be there than somewhere else. If that's true, then maybe those detentions

need to be more about figuring out why a student doesn't want to be with their peers and/or playing.

- Do communicate with parents/guardians. There should be no surprise about anything, whether it's a grade, a punishment, a consequence, or a reward. I'm a big fan of email but I know it's not the best way of communicating home. Emails can be misunderstood. Tone isn't always conveyed accurately. Phone calls are much better. Being able to talk about a student's strengths as well as areas of need is my primary focus when calling home. I don't love "sunshine" calls (when a teacher calls to gush about how great a kid is). I understand the logic behind the idea but as a parent myself, I know my kid is great; I don't need you to tell me that (I also know I'm probably in the minority here). I'm a bigger fan of praising every student directly. When I call home, I make sure I have useful things to say and suggestions for the help I need from home as well as positive things happening in class with the student at the centre.
- Behavior that in any shape or form, to any degree, doesn't fit with the teacher's expectations should be addressed. I would suggest, however, before doling out punishment, you take some time to consider what might be causing the behavior (stressful family situation, hunger, lack of sleep, something you said or asked them to do).
- If you're desperate and need to get an immediate response, using an authoritative voice, count, out loud, to three. Believe it or not, counting works just as well on six-year-olds as it does on eighteen-year-olds. "I'm giving you to the count of three. One, two..."
- Seating plans are powerful, so use them wisely. I mentioned earlier that I'm not a fan of seating plans upfront. I used them, more so in my earlier days as a teacher, but I moved away from them as I gained a better understanding of building community. There is a time and place for seating plans. I use them for activities when I want to move students into groupings that work better for my lesson plan, with consideration for student preferences and the feeling of comfort. For example, I wouldn't yank a timid student from their only friend in an attempt to push them into making new friends. I would work with that student on their personal goals and if they say that they'd like to get more comfortable with working with people they don't know, that's when I push. I also use seating plans as a temporary fix for a class that can't seem to control their behavior. It has immediate effect and can absolutely kill the vibe in a room, so I only use it when things have gone to the extreme in terms of behavior management.
- A quiet class isn't always an engaged class, so don't be afraid of a little noise. A noisy room usually means that students are working on something that interests and excites them. There is a time and place for quiet. On days where we need quiet time, I make sure the class understands my expectations. I rarely expect a class to be silent for an extended period of time. Sometimes that just happens naturally as students are busy working, but I like a noisy room. To me, that means students are engaged. And I confirm they're engaged because I'm moving around the room interacting during that time, redirecting if they get off task.
- Avoid making assumptions about anything or anyone. You know why.
- Use statements that start with, "I feel" rather than, "You are" or "That's the way it is so deal with it." Or "I'm the boss, that's why." Instead start

with, "I feel like this might not be working the way I planned." Or "I feel like this might be getting frustrating for us to do."

I'm not saying you have to memorize all of this information in order to be successful. You bought my book, and it's there for reference any time you need it. What I am saying is that if you practice these things, even one or two every day, they'll start to come naturally. When they come naturally, you'll be able to walk into any classroom, or, even any space with twenty-plus people, instantaneously assess what needs doing, then start doing it without conscious thought. It might take some time but it's worth it in the end, not only for your stress level and sanity but also for the students in your care.

In Short

- Teach students about expectations specific to your classroom, what they mean, their purpose, and what the consequences of breaking those expectations will be.
- Consider working with students to create the classroom expectations. Meet them where they are with their previous experiences and build expectations by including them in the discussion.
- Model the behavior you wish to see from your students.
- Be consistent in following classroom expectations and consequences.
- Establish routines so students know what to expect every day and work with them on being flexible if surprises pop up that are out of your control.
- Go back to page 54 and read "General Tips for Sanity". It's a list of dos and don'ts when it comes to expectations. It's not long, I promise, but it is incredibly useful. If you're going to cherry-pick parts of this book, it's a must read.

STEP 3

Get Your Paperwork in Order

I bet you weren't counting on a section about paperwork, were you? This isn't a bait and switch, although I do love talking about lesson planning and assessment/evaluation just for the fun of it. I'm including paperwork because being organized, transparent, and fair must be built into your daily practice, which means everything you do with your students should be intentional (to the degree that it can be). Sometimes things come out of nowhere, hijacking your plans, and you have to switch course on the spot. It's better, when that happens, to have a plan to begin with so you know your destination no matter what might take you off course.

I promise you, if you have a solid handle on the paperwork, you'll succeed at classroom management in any room full of humans needing direction.

The Trifecta of Success

A) Content/Curriculum Plan(s) + B) Assessment/Evaluation Destination(s) = C) Successful Classroom Management

Just as you shouldn't walk into a classroom without a plan for the space, you shouldn't walk in without a lesson/unit and an assessment/evaluation plan.

Why? Because if you enter the space feeling disorganized, trying to wing it, your students will also feel disorganized, and that feeling leads to stress and anxiety, which often feeds into behavior issues. That's not to say that you can't pull it off once or twice, maybe more with experience, but if you're with a class for the long haul, you can't keep winging it. You must plan.

Content/Curriculum Plan(s)

You shouldn't and really, if I'm being honest, can't properly write a lesson plan or unit plan or any plan without knowing the curriculum. Luckily, we live in a time where most curriculum can be found online and it doesn't need to be memorized because you can (and should) refer to it whenever you want.

Start with the curriculum!

Before you start your planning, you must investigate what the expectations or standards are for the subject you're teaching. The curriculum is usually available online, by province/state/region, and by grade, and is organized into both overall expectations/standards and specific expectations/standards (in Ontario and many other provinces/countries). In general, our job is to teach the specific expectations and evaluate the overall expectations. (*If it's different where you are, reach out to the powers that be and find out what the standards/expectations are, then use them for planning.)

Curriculum should act as the goalposts or route markings on the way to our destination.

If you look at the Ontario curriculum, you may feel overwhelmed. You'll see lists and lists of specific expectations and wonder, How in the heck will I be able to teach all of this? I could write a book about the nitty-gritty of planning but, for now, I'll say you're going to make your life easier by bundling expectations together.

If you're in an elementary classroom, you're going to practice writing skills through science lab reports while doing science experiments so that you can tackle more expectations at once. You're going to teach about Indigenous Treaties while practicing reading skills. You're going to apply math knowledge to social studies by measuring wood for a lean-to in survival camping.

For secondary classrooms, you're going to gather a few expectations together for your subject and create a lesson that meets those expectations. This will sometimes have to be a (strict) sequential bundling because in many subject areas one concept needs to be taught before another concept can be understood. Some subject areas follow a more rigid sequence. For example, in math, you need to know how various subsets of number systems are defined before you can understand how to create a set of numbers and then compare them to other sets of numbers to find similarities and differences (Mathematics, Ontario Curriculum). There are some subjects that will follow time periods in a logical, sequential way where students will need to know what happened between, say, 1914 and 1929 before they can fully grasp the impact on the period of 1929 to 1945. In other subject areas there is more flexibility to jump around, especially if there are expectations around Inquiry Learning (asking questions, researching, critical analysis, finding conclusions, communicating to an audience). You could end up cycling through the inquiry curriculum expectations a few times in one term by focusing on different areas of study. For other subjects, you'll be able to blend expectations together from different strands and cycle through many of them more than once. For example, in an English novel study unit, you'd probably focus on language conventions, understanding, and responding to text and comprehension strategies, organizing content and reflecting on learning. (English, Ontario Curriculum)

Starting with the curriculum is typically a non-negotiable in teaching. If there's curriculum available, set out by the government/employer, you'll need to use it.

If there isn't curriculum, as in the case of Locally Developed or specialized Student Services/Special Education classes, then you're going to be creating lesson plans that are unique to each individual student in front of you, usually by incorporating aspects of their IEP (Individual Education Plan). You and the student (where possible), along with parents/guardians, will set goals in a specific subject or general area of need, then you'll incorporate content and teach skills that help them achieve those goals.

Assessment/Evaluation Destination(s)

The other thing you absolutely need to know before you start the nitty-gritty part of lesson planning is where you're headed. You need to know in advance, for the unit and for the lesson plans, what ways you'll be assessing students (teacher/self/peer) and what you'll be evaluating (process/final product). There should be no surprises to the students (parents/guardians) or to you. You can't make it up as you go along because: 1) that's incredibly unfair to students; 2) you won't be meeting your professional obligations; and 3) you must explicitly teach anything you're going to grade, which means you must know what you'll be grading ahead of time so you can teach it. I'll dig into this more shortly.

Make it your common practice to ensure there are no surprises when it comes to assessment and evaluation.

What Goes into a Lesson Plan?

Let me first say that a lesson plan doesn't need to be fancy, typed, or even on 8.5 x 11 paper. It can be messy, with notes scribbled everywhere, as long as it's legible to you and contains the key elements that make it a complete lesson plan. This of course is something you should check with your employer to ensure you're following their recommended guidelines and standards, but in general the lesson/unit plan can take whatever format best works for you. It's a tool for you to use, not something students or parents will ever see.

I'll admit that for a while I was doing my lesson plans on giant, long sticky notes. It was convenient for me because I could jot down what was working and what wasn't, then when I typed it up (for official, teacher evaluation reasons) I would make it fancy. At the end of the lesson, I'd go back and incorporate the daily changes needed with notes on contingencies, what expectations worked, which ones might work better, etc. But that was back in the day when computers weren't in every classroom and I didn't have a laptop with me at all times. Now, I just take notes on a doc using a template I create with the categories I'm going to list below.

I still use sticky notes but they're for my daily plans and usually look more like a checklist.

Note: Keep in mind that an employer can ask to see your plans at any point on any day, even if it's not during an evaluation, so you need to be comfortable with them looking at plans that aren't pretty. If that makes your skin crawl then sticky notes are not for you.

Also, most school boards require that you have completely planned the unit you're currently teaching, and any units that came before the one you're teaching should be complete as well. Any units to come can be rough ideas. The reasoning for this is that you may need to change unit plans down the road based on what happens as you're teaching a unit.

If students aren't grasping ideas, then you might end up taking longer in one area or you might need to reteach/review concepts in the next unit more than you thought you would so adjustments will need to be made to reflect the needs of your students. Do some teachers have complete units ready to go at the beginning of the year for the whole year or semester? Absolutely. That's one of the "perks" of teaching the same grade/subject over and over again. Should those same teachers make changes to suit the needs of the students in front of them rather than stick to what is set in stone? Also, yes.

I get it, we need to find ways to cut down our workload so we have a life beyond marking, prepping, and teaching. I'm not saying you have to reinvent the wheel every year, term, or semester of your career, I'm saying you should tweak things so your students benefit from the learning and find success in what you teach.

Your unit plans will span a larger period of time than your lesson plans but there's no recipe that works for every class all the time. Some units might be two weeks, some a month, while other units span three months and umbrella other units happening at the same time.

Unit plans don't need to be super-specific if you want to leave the detail to your lesson plans. Some teachers work better with a brief overview of the unit ideas (expectations, assessment/evaluations, accommodations, etc).

I create a daily plan template in my Google drive for each new term with specific information just in case I'm away. It's ready to go with a little tweaking to add what I want accomplished while I'm absent. It's handy to have this ready for times when I'm too sick to think clearly.

Then, in elementary, though I know secondary teachers who use this principle, there are daily plans. This is where you create a working agenda for your day, including overall targets for each teaching chunk you are scheduled for. I leave daily plans for supply teachers so they have details of what we're doing, who will help them, how our rules work, who needs specific accommodations, what to expect, contingency plans, and important phone numbers they might need.

As I've already mentioned, this isn't a book about planning, this is a book about classroom *management,* and I realize that I'm getting into the weeds a bit. While all of these components are important, I'm going to focus closely on the lesson plan because that usually has the grand scheme that most impacts students and their emotional/physical/spiritual well-being.

Complete lesson plans are usually required for three to five days in the future (this is just in case you have an extended absence and aren't able to lesson-plan immediately) and you should have one completed for every day that has already happened in a term. Again, this is because we want to ensure we're creating relevant plans for the students currently in front of us and be able to show where we've been and where we're headed.

This might look different in different boards/countries. You'll need to check with your board to be sure. Unions and administration will have their own take on these things as well. Usually, they're aligned with whatever the employer has set out, but not always.

I've worked with principals who want *all* the paperwork, scripted even, down to what I'll be saying to students. And I've worked with principals who barely look at my paperwork and are more interested in what they observe, what I tell them, and how I answer their questions.

While it's tempting to have lesson and unit plans (day plans even) that stay unchanged year after year no matter who enters your classroom in order to reduce workload, it's not always great for students. No change means your lesson/unit plans grow stagnant and may lose relevance to your new classes. What worked ten years ago probably doesn't work now and arguing that "This is the way it's always been done" is a recipe for upholding systemic barriers and unfair teaching practices. If we cling to the same ole, we lose opportunities to engage students with material that they see themselves in and connect to.

Sticking with the old and comfortable is going to stifle your growth as an educator as well. We're lifelong learners, aren't we? That means we should keep ourselves engaged and try new things every once in a while. Changing things up here and there is good for everyone, even if it's a lot of work upfront. It makes teaching more exciting and engaging for us, which means the same for students. If you're bored, they're bored.

If you're bored, they're bored.

Parts of a Lesson Plan

Strategy: Minds On/Lesson Starter/Hook/Setting the Tone

- Whatever you want to call it, you need to have a way to bring students into the lesson with some kind of activity that gets them thinking and, possibly, moving around the space.
  - This can be done by watching a (short) video (no longer than five minutes) that's funny, heartwarming, educational — whatever, that will set the tone for the lesson.
  - It can be done with mind benders and riddles or some kind of puzzle.
  - It can be an inquiry question linked to the lesson topic that gets students thinking: For example, what would you say if you could talk with animals and they could talk back in our language?
  - It can be done with a picture or photo to generate ideas.
- There are endless "minds-on" activities you can do. They can be simple or more complicated, as long as the understanding is that the activity is supposed to be an easy and engaging entry point for students. Hitting them with something that's too difficult and that takes too long will stymie engagement. That's not to say you can't have a difficult problem or mystery to solve that acts as a challenge for the day/week/month/year. In fact, you can design a lot of fun term/semester-long mysteries that students attempt to solve as you move through the units and they gain hints/clues. That being said, in general, I never let a minds-on last more than five–ten minutes. Sometimes I pose a question or have students brainstorm questions that we make predictions about and come back to later in the lesson. It doesn't need to be heavy. It just needs to be relevant, engaging, and something that springboards students into the next stage of the lesson.

Strategy: Action Sequence

- Remember, we're focused on curriculum expectations here, so there's a specific point to what we're teaching. I advocate for minimal teacher *talking* time (avoid the sage-on-the-stage mentality — step away from the podium and stop putting students to sleep) and maximum time for student *doing*.
- People learn best when they're actively engaging in some way, which includes my favorite, reciprocal teaching. Students who learn a concept or skill, then teach it to someone else (might be me, might be someone at home, might be a classmate) have a better understanding of the concept/skill and they get a nice little self-esteem boost for being a leader, a teacher, and a knower of things. Not only does this increase engagement but when

people are happy and feel good about themselves they're less likely to act out with unwanted behavior.

- Whatever the action sequence is (the "doing" part of the lesson) it should be broken up into manageable chunks — maximum ten minutes of teacher instructions/teaching/talking, fifteen-thirty minutes of student driven learning, group or independent work, five minutes of further teacher direction/teaching, fifteen minutes of something, repeat, etc. Breaking up the action allows for small victories and makes tasks much more manageable and less overwhelming.

  You can use models like:
  - A five-part workshop model which includes a mini-lesson, then students go off to do independent work. While students work, the teacher checks in/gives feedback to individuals or leads small groups in focused learning. If required, the teacher will pause independent work to give a full-class clarification or mini-mini-lesson. End with some kind of sharing or consolidation.
  - Or you can browse sites like TVO Learn (TVOlearn.com) which has ideas to springboard from using a simple hook, action, consolidation model. *In fact, they have complete lesson plans that derive from Ontario curriculum for most grades and subjects.
  - Or you can take inspiration from many Multi-Language Learner teachers who use the PPP model — Present, Practice, Produce — which opens up many options for who presents, what is presented, how it is presented, practicing a skill or using a skill to digest content, then applying those skills and information to produce something.
  - Or you can look into the Penny Kittle model of structuring lessons which can look something like: Book Talk, Reading Time, Quick Write, Sharing, Mini-Lesson, Create/Work Time.
  - Yes, I know, the last two are language-based suggestions but I'm only asking you to be open to inspiration and ideas, not commit to a prenup or marriage contract. You might find that there's a fantastic lesson plan model in an unlikely place.
- The pace should match the class dynamic. If you have a high-energy group, you may need to put breaks in to bring the energy down a little here and there so that no one goes off the rails and escalates to unwanted behavior. If you have a quiet group, you'll need to amp things up strategically so excitement builds, but not so much that students feel overwhelmed.
- This is how working the space and knowing your students come into play — you need to know what motivates your students to do things. What is their currency? Then you need to figure out how to use that knowledge to strategically plan and anticipate possible derailments in order to reduce the chances of classroom management issues.

See? There is a point to all that preplanning!

Strategy: Consolidation/The End

- You need to wrap things up at the end of a day's lesson. It need not take more than two to five minutes. Ask students to revisit learning goals or an inquiry question the lesson started with. You can survey answers, do a ticket-out-the-door (have students reflect on three things they learned), ask some questions (or brainstorm with the class) to continue the next day, build reflection in: what are you still wondering, how far did you get, what are your goals for tomorrow?...etc.

- Lesson plans sometimes take days to wrap up, in which case, at the end of each day/class, you'll do a mini-consolidation about what was covered that day, then pick up where you left off the next day — like a cliffhanger to the next chapter. If you've managed to hook students with the learning on day one, they'll be eager to continue on day two.
- Each day of the learning cycle, you'll need another minds-on, action, and consolidation but the curriculum expectations continue to the next day(s) until the learning cycle is complete. I've never had a lesson last more than five days and that was only because it led into a project. Usually a lesson will be one to three days.
- A unit plan is the overall goal for the entire (week/multi-week) unit. It's written as an overview of everything that will be covered during that time, the assessment goals, and ultimately what the evaluation project(s) will be.
- There are a lot of samples and templates for lesson plans out there. While I love the idea of using AI or teacher-pay-teacher sites for inspiration, we must keep in mind that our plans need to be rooted in the curriculum (whatever that may be for your employer) and should be suited to the students in front of us.

Tips and Tricks: Lesson Planning Survival Skills

- Embrace curiosity. Give students room to explore topics of interest and be okay with not knowing the answers yourself. It's fine to say, "I don't know; let's do some research." Or, "I'm not sure how to answer that, I'll get back to you." Or, "How about you do some research and teach me about it?"
- Inquiry is a winner. I love using inquiry and project-based learning in my lesson plans. Helping students hone their natural curiosity into compelling questions enhances and nurtures their creativity. Giving them choice to explore topics that interest them also makes learning more engaging. There are so many ways to use inquiry (I could write another book about it) and luckily, there is also an unending supply of resources out there with information. It's not a free-for-all, as some may believe. Inquiry takes planning and scaffolding to teach students how to move from a fully teacher-guided inquiry project to more independence, but it's so worth it. The level of engagement I've experienced from students during inquiry projects is unmatched. They take pride in their work, are excited about the outcomes, and are eager to share. If you want to see the ultimate project-based learning examples, do a web search on genius hour videos. The things you'll see will amaze you!
- Let the students teach you. Whether it's about technology, music, social media, math, or dog behaviors, be open to students teaching you things. Not only is this a great way to get to know them, but you can pump up their self-esteem by letting them know that their knowledge is valuable. It's totally okay for you to not know everything. Giving your students room to educate, to teach everyone, is a way to engage them in learning.
- Understand that behavior issues might be a result of something in your unit/lesson plan. Talking to students and getting their feedback through-

out a learning cycle is helpful because it might be a *you* problem, not a *them* problem, when it comes to their behavior. What I mean is, you may unknowingly design a lesson around something that is triggering to students, which then leads to unwanted behavior. It could look like disengagement, outbursts, tears, anger, etc. What you think is a wonderful idea might be torture for students. Having an ear to their concerns and being open to switching things up is a huge step toward preventing classroom management issues.

Assessment and Evaluation

Whether or not you realize it, when you assign a grade to something, the learning stops. In our merit-driven world, a grade signifies the end of learning, and the higher the grade the better we feel about ourselves. There's not a lot we can do to change that in the immediate future but I know there are teachers actively trying to shift us away from grading. If you're interested in learning more, you should do an internet search on the "ungrading movement" Or "gradeless classrooms".

Because it's a judgement, yours exclusively, you must be very careful in how you use grades.

Grades are powerful.

They can motivate a student to do well and they can devastate a student's well-being for a lifetime.

Don't ever underestimate the impact of assessment and evaluation.

The purpose of assessment and evaluation is to improve student learning.

As I mentioned before, the purpose of assessment is to improve student learning. At the end of a learning cycle (usually at the end of a unit) we typically evaluate using the evidence we've collected through our assessments.

We grade using the overall expectations provided by the government in our curriculum documents (this might vary depending on where you teach in the world). Those overall expectations are a cumulative summary of the learning that needs to happen over the course of time you have with your students.

What the curriculum usually doesn't demand is *how* we teach a subject and *how* we assess during the learning and evaluate at the end of the learning.

That means we have a lot of freedom for professional judgement. In my opinion, professional judgment needs to be anchored in evidence, which is why documentation of our conversations and observations is super important. More on this later.

Believe it or not, assessment and evaluation have a tremendous impact on classroom management. Because we put such high value on grades as a society, we put emphasis on the end result rather than the process of learning and the concept of failing being a necessary component of learning — low-stakes failing. When a student repeatedly achieves low grades, their self-esteem nosedives, which, in turn makes them feel crappy and can lead to behavior issues, disengagement, apathy, etc.

What this means for you is that a tremendous amount of consideration must go into planning how you're going to assess, then evaluate. Which is why you need to plan ahead, right to the end of the term, so you know what you'll ultimately be grading. There should be no surprises for anyone, including you, when it comes to your assessment/evaluation plans.

Assessments should happen throughout a learning cycle, during the process of learning, which allows for failures and setbacks with low stakes, meaning no marks that stick. This gives students time to practice what they've learned in a safe and supportive way before they reach the final stage of the process and submit a completed draft. During the process, you should embed time to give feedback to each student, catch them if they've mis-stepped, redirect them, and ensure that you're guiding them to success.

As noted earlier, you should not use gotchas. For example, a gotcha would be knowing a student is making a mistake with a project but letting them go without feedback so they learn "natural consequences". Natural consequences aren't natural in a learning environment when you withhold information from someone. That's why feedback from you, check-ins, and redirects are important. If, after you've done that, a student still proceeds with an idea against your advice or doesn't take feedback you've given, then the natural consequences are fair. And you might just be proven wrong, especially when it comes to radical ideas, which is okay as well.

What wouldn't be fair would be if you proceeded to lower a mark only because the student didn't take your advice. That would be a nasty move. Unjustifiable and cruel. Not a good use of professional judgment.

You should build in time for peers to give feedback. Of course, you'll need to teach your students how to be effective at giving constructive peer feedback. You should also build in teaching time about how to self-reflect and self-edit.

Teach it, model it, then give time to practice with no penalty. Don't grade the practice runs.

During the assessment stage, you should spend time recording the conversations you have with students. Not word for word — that's too time-consuming — but a recap in point form is good. Remember how I said that I had a way of doing "marking" on the move so I didn't have to sit at my desk to do it? This is the documentation you'll later use to inform your professional judgment, and now is the time to do it.

Jot down what feedback you're giving and what you notice about the student's work. Document it. What observations do you have about the work your student has done so far? What expectations are being met already, which ones need more bolstering and practice time? You could carry a list of expectations that students are learning and gather information about how well they're progressing in different areas by checking off the list.

You're collecting data that can inform your evaluation of student learning as long as it's done in a way that is not punitive. This is not a time for you to capture what the student is doing wrong, rather what suggestions you're making to improve the student work and how the student is incorporating those suggestions. These conversations and observations can be used to help determine a final grade, but only to boost marks. You're not recording behavior here and you're definitely not using behavior as a grade determination.

If you've let students know that you're evaluating them during certain conversations/observations and you've been clear about success criteria — what they need to do to achieve their desired mark — then you can work evaluation checkpoints into the process. For example, you might want to include three formal group meetings during a project where students share some part of their work with small groups. During that conversation, they will have certain criteria to complete that you will be assigning a grade to. You might also be observing how well they act as a leader in the group with a separate set of curriculum-specific criteria that they are trying to achieve, perhaps related to communication.

Another way to use this data would be in a situation where a student shows learning during an informal activity but bombs the final evaluation. For example, I'm observing group conversations when I overhear Jai talking about electrical currents with his group in a way that clearly shows he understands and knows how to apply the curriculum expectation we're covering. This is evidence of his learning that I can use later to show that he understands a concept and knows how to adapt his thinking in new contexts. That way, if Jai does poorly on the unit test a week later, I know it isn't because he doesn't know the answers but because of something else, like test anxiety or lack of sleep, or hunger; or, perhaps, the test itself is poorly worded.

Note: Mistakes happen. Sometimes, something we create for an evaluation is just plain bad. If you see that a lot of students are stuck in one area or if more than three students are failing an evaluation (e.g., a test) then it's probably the test that is the problem, not the students. Reflect on that, make changes, fix the problem, and don't punish the students for it. It's okay to say, "Hey, that test wasn't capturing what I wanted to capture from you all; let's try this again a different way."

You could pair a test with a conversation. Some students do much better explaining what they mean orally rather than in writing. If you've been tracking conversations and observations, you can also use your professional judgement to supplement the test results with successes you've already seen from students through the unit. The test results alone don't have to be the final mark.

Remember, it's not a bad thing for your students to succeed.

A few years ago, I was teaching speechwriting and delivery to a class and we spent time learning about different kinds of speeches and how to use body language and other soft skills to effectively deliver a message. A lot of the time during the process of learning was spent with students working in small groups and partners. While they were working on their speeches, I'd set days aside where I would have conversations, give feedback, and sometimes just observe discussion in their groups. If I was going to be using these conversation and observation notes to inform my judgement on final grades, I would make sure students were aware ahead of time so they understood the value I was putting on a certain activity.

That year I had a student who was very nervous to give a speech in front of the class but she had set a goal to improve her comfort level with presentation delivery and was determined to do it before the term was over. During the process work, we often met to have conversations about what might work better and how she was progressing. I documented how she was doing with her understanding of the skills I'd taught her or skills she'd taught herself and how she was applying them in new ways. I also documented times that she practiced her speech to herself and to small groups, recording all of the things she was doing really well and what expectations she was hitting dead on. I gave her feedback all the way through.

On the day of her speech, she got up at the front of the class, started to talk with great enthusiasm, confidence clearly high, then, like a spectacular card trick, she fumbled her cue cards, sending them flying in all directions. The class helped her pick them up but she had no quick way to put them back in order. She panicked, stumbled her way through the rest of her speech, face scarlet, and by the time it was over, she looked totally defeated.

If I had been the type of teacher who believed in one-and-done evaluations, valuing the product (the speech) above the process, then her mark on the speech would have been abysmal and she likely would never have wanted to give another speech again.

Because I'm not that type of teacher, and I'd experienced her giving the speech flawlessly already more than once, I knew how hard she'd worked to ensure that she would succeed on speech day and how she'd already met the expectations to near perfection. I gave her the rubric with my notes (back then it was all on paper), letting her know that she earned the grade she was aiming for (A+), and we talked about what she might have done differently if she were to give another speech. She reflected, said she'd number her cue cards for sure, and later on in the term, when given the choice of making a speech or something else, she chose to make another speech. I credit her bravery to attempt Round Two with the flexibility I showed, proving that she could trust me to have her best interests in mind, knowing that I would use all the data available to ensure her success.

The most important thing, in my opinion, is the learning that happens throughout a project and by recording conversations and observations, noting achievements all the way, I'd given this student multiple opportunities to show me what she had learned.

You may not feel comfortable or confident enough yet to use your professional judgement that way, in which case you might decide to give that student a second opportunity to give her speech, on a different day, once she has had a chance to work up her courage.

I didn't see the point in a repeat performance for that project when I knew there would be other opportunities coming up where the student could choose to try public speaking again in a different context. Also, with so much emphasis put on the process for this project, the final product was less important.

Whatever you do, these conversations and observations are meant to enhance student achievement and should not be used in a punitive way. Recording behavior issues to be used as grade determination doesn't support student success. You shouldn't be observing Iris acting out and use that as a means to lower her mark. This includes attendance. Just because Matthew is late doesn't mean he should lose marks.

Grades that are used to moderate behavior are not being used fairly. This practice, while common, is not supported by curriculum documents and doesn't do what you think it does. Using grades to punish doesn't promote learning, it promotes an escalation of behavior and disengagement. Using grades to take away a field trip opportunity or sporting event can isolate a student. Not only does that hurt a student's self-esteem by pointing out to everyone that they are "below average" but it can lead them to act out. In my opinion, if the field trip or sporting event is so easily discarded for one student over grades, what is the purpose of it overall? If it's teaching something, then it should be available to teach everybody or it's not an equitable experience. If it's a reward for good behavior and some students are excluded, even when poor behavior can be caused by things we as teachers do, things that happen inside or outside the classroom, things out of a student's control, then that's just cruel.

How Do We Measure Learning?

You need to plan how you'll ultimately evaluate, place a mark on, the learning a student has achieved. This requires some way of measuring the "final project" or evidence of learning. This could be measured with a rubric, a checklist, a sliding scale, etc. Whatever method you use, you must give clear expectations and goals and, for the love of salted caramel, make sure you explicitly teach whatever you're grading. If you don't teach them how to do "it", then how will they know how to do "it"?

Some things I believe in the name of fairness:

- You can't expect students to read your mind, "I'll know an A+ when I see one." And you shouldn't be moving the goalposts either. "This wasn't really what I was looking for from you." "I was expecting more detail/effort [something arbitrary that you make up because you don't want this student to achieve a high mark] from you."
- Students *absolutely* <u>should</u> be able to achieve perfect scores. There are no standards that dictate you must cap your grades at 80% or some other arbitrary number. I've worked with teachers who determine that perfection is impossible and no student will ever achieve a mark of more than 90% or A+. If that's true, then why are we grading out of 100% or using standards like A, B, C to determine grades? If the cap is a 90% then that is the highest score, which makes it a perfect score, doesn't it? If it's not a perfect score, then where does that 10% go? Does it just disappear? Does the teacher skim off the top for themselves? If this is the accepted practice then how in the world is our assessment and evaluation fair, transparent, and equitable? It's not, so this practice needs to go.
- Be clear about your late/missed work policy. You might have one that is school-based, and/or you likely have one that is board-based. Remember that there are legitimate reasons why a student doesn't complete work. Some of it is on you. Some of it is on them. Some of it can be linked to things that are out of both of your control.
- Keep in mind that if you give a lot of assignments, you give yourself a lot of homework. It is my belief that part of your professional duty requires that you mark things quickly and get them back to students so that they can use the feedback from the returned assignment to move forward. Just so you know, it absolutely kills me to write what I just wrote: if you're giving "feedback" at the end of the learning cycle, then you're basically saying, "Better luck next time!" But there won't be a next time in this exact way so "Good luck applying my very specific-to-this-assignment feedback on your next very different assignment". It seems unfair to me and pointless for everyone, but it is absolutely common practice, which is why I've included it.
- If you're assessing throughout, giving feedback during the learning and not withholding tips for success, then the final grade becomes a manageable stake (rather than a high stake) because students already know what they need to do to get the grades they want. Then, if they use the feedback before handing the assignment in, (surprise!) they achieve their goals.

When you put all evaluation possibilities into a one-and-done, one-shot opportunity, you're limiting a student to showing you their learning in one event at one point in time. This is typically done as timed writing, tests (quizzes), and presentations. Students might be able to do the task perfectly in class during practice time when the pressure is off but when the actual test/performance comes around, they panic and don't perform at their best. Does that mean that they didn't learn anything? Did they fail to achieve the expectations? Not necessarily. It can mean on that day, at that time, they weren't performing their best. Period. Any number of influences can impact a one-and-done evaluation. Lack of sleep, hunger, anxiety, missed learning opportunities, etc. Things that are out of a student's control.

If, instead of one-and-done evaluations, you value the process of learning more than the final product, then some of the pressure is off so students don't need to worry so much about the perfect final project or one-shot test when all throughout the process they're showing you their learning in different ways. You just need to be listening and watching for it. That reduces your marking at the end of the learning cycle because you've been keeping track of student achievement all the way through. It means that if a student ends up not handing in a final project for unexpected reasons out of their control (or even reasons that people perceive are in a student's control, like procrastination and time management and perfectionism), they can still feel good about what they have already achieved and you can feel confident that they did, in fact, learn what you wanted them to learn.

Allowing this improves engagement because students know they're going to succeed and feel proud of their work. They won't give up when facing challenges because they'll learn that challenges are a part of the process and that "failure" comes with an invitation to try again.

And yes, it also means your class average will be high. There is absolutely nothing wrong with students succeeding gloriously. Spectacularly even!

Successful Classroom Management

What does this all have to do with classroom management?

If you're organized, know what you're doing each day, and have a plan for where you're headed that makes sense to students, they will feel confident that you're in charge of things. You're the leader with the plan and that brings comfort and safety.

Even if a lesson plan doesn't go well, or it completely bombs, or an evaluation you've created isn't working for the students in front of you, that doesn't mean you've failed. It means it's time for growing and learning, which comes with setbacks and mistakes. Modeling for students that you're not going to be derailed by a mistake and instead you're going to try a different way is what teaching is all about. It actually inspires innovation and creativity to find a different approach and solution, which, in my opinion, is modeling what it's like to live in the real world. And I *know* we're all about preparing students for the "real world". Being prepared, even when it doesn't work out the way you've envisioned, shows students that you're human, and part of being a human is admitting when something isn't going the way you've planned, then coming at it in different ways.

Being a leader with a plan projects confidence and confidence invites respect. Respect that has been earned reduces classroom management issues.

Having fair, transparent, and equitable assessment and evaluation practices reduces anxiety for students, which in turn reduces triggers for behavior. Helping students understand that in the safe space of your classroom will give them opportunities to shine, opportunities to boost their confidence, to celebrate learning and to tackle setbacks with enthusiasm. With all of that, you'll have fewer classroom management issues.

Making sure that no student feels isolated because they think they're dumb, or left out because they didn't perform well on a test, or inadequate as a human because of a grade, means you'll have fewer classroom management struggles.

Happy, safe, and comfortable people don't lash out

Happy, safe, and comfortable people don't lash out. Any behavior you see or hear is a result of something. It's the canary in the mineshaft. It's a clue that something else is going on. While you can't typically control what happens outside of your sphere, you can control what a student walks into for the time you have them. That goes a long way in preventing behavior that disrupts the goals of the day.

In Short

- You need to be intentional with your planning so there are minimal surprises for you or your students. This includes not only your daily lesson/unit plans but whatever assessment and evaluation tasks you will be asking students to complete.
- Remember that we are always being watched by our students, so modeling disorganization can lead to stress and anxiety for our students. Stress and anxiety can lead to behavior issues.
- Know your curriculum. Start by designing plans with curriculum expectations as the goalposts.
- For classes with no government-mandated curriculum, you're going to create plans based on the unique needs of your students, like using their IEP (Individual Education Plan) to guide creation of the goalposts.
- You must explicitly teach anything you're going to grade. If you're grading tardiness, guess what? You need to teach about it first. But don't grade tardiness unless it's in the curriculum…which it's not. At least not in my region.
- A lesson/unit plan can take whatever form best works for you. It's a tool for you to use, not something students or parents will ever see.
- There are three components of an effective lesson plan: Minds On/Lesson Starter/Hook/Setting the Tone; Action Sequence; Consolidation.
- You need to know what motivates your students to do things. What is their currency? Then you need to figure out how to use that knowledge to strategically plan and anticipate possible derailments in order to reduce the chances of classroom management issues.
- Remember, when you assign a grade to something, the learning stops. Our goal in grading is to support student learning and growth.
- Assessments should happen during the process of learning, which allows for failures and setbacks with low stakes, meaning no marks that stick, giving students time to practice.
- Use conversations and observations alongside your professional judgement to determine final grades. These should not be used in a punitive way, ever, though. Whatever you do, these conversations and observations are meant to enhance student achievement.

STEP 4

Be a Storyteller

Imagine you're new to a school, low teacher in the pecking order of timetabling, gifted a stacked class, with more students than the classroom can hold. You already know all about the high rollers because every teacher you've met so far has warned you about their "behavior". This particular cohort has a reputation for being wild, disengaged, low achievers and always timetabled together for some mysterious reason.

You walk into the classroom, the students start tumbling in, rough-housing, loud, looking at you as if you're the next obstacle to dominate. Even though you're an unknown entity to them because you're new to the school, this isn't their first rodeo.

They fight over seats.

You're organized. You've followed the steps. You show them the seating plan.

They show you how much they hate that idea. They snicker. They make rude comments. They take the seats you've assigned but move their chairs fractionally closer to their friends just to show you who's boss.

They wait for your next move, impatience crackling like static.

Don't Panic

The scenario I just painted for you was my first experience with a class of my own. I was nervous and excited and, as prepared as I thought I was, I wasn't remotely ready for this group of students. The odds were stacked against me before I even entered the building. The students had years of experience under their belts. I had none.

The first day didn't go well. Neither did the second day. Students put minimal effort into the get-to-know you surveys and activities I'd been excited about. They didn't want to participate, thought my ideas were stupid, pointless, a waste of their time. I could see why the other teachers had said what they had. These students were not happy to be in my class. They didn't want to do the work I'd planned. They weren't listening to me while I was teaching. Their dismissal of me was something I hadn't anticipated. I think, like a lot of inexperienced teachers, I walked into the classroom expecting that being *the teacher* alone would grant me respect.

I was sorely mistaken and the students were efficient in cutting my ego down.

It was awful. Disheartening. I felt I'd made a terrible mistake in choosing to be a teacher. Obviously, I sucked at it.

Then, out of sheer desperation, I remembered something I'd seen work in another class. During one of my teaching placements while in teachers' college, I'd had a very hands-off associate teacher. He showed me the "ropes" for one day, then abandoned me to his classes after that. Talk about trial by fire!

In that one day, though, I watched him masterfully capture a rowdy class's attention with a story about a trip he took to a mountain where he was going to camp. It was a thrilling story about hitchhiking (not recommended) and swerving trucks, mountain climbing and snow. I was riveted and so were the students. Some asked questions but mostly they all sat and listened.

While he was telling the story, he was drawing up a seating plan. He'd warned the class twice about not getting work done and being too off task and had threatened a seating plan to separate friends from one another so that things would settle down. All the while that he was telling his fantastic story, he was also drawing out the desk layout on a piece of paper and moving students from one area to another. It took about ten minutes and by the time he was finished with this story, the seating plan was complete and the class was quiet. He let them know what their new seating assignment would be, following through with consequences of their previous behavior because he knew that, if he didn't act, as soon as he asked students to get to work again, they'd be off task. Even though there were a lot of moans and groans, they got up, moved, then got to work.

It seemed like a miracle to me. He'd given ample warning. He hadn't gotten angry or frustrated. He'd calmly, patiently, changed the tone of the room and given students a reset with his story. Then, with little fanfare, he followed through on consequences and the students complied.

It was expert-level classroom management in action and I was lucky enough to experience it that one time. He showed me that there was a way of bringing chaos to calm without raising my voice or throwing down threats.

A lightbulb went off and I thought... *Hey! I can tell stories!*

So, back to my first experience in my own classroom with a bunch of students who were all very consistent in their unruly behavior from day to day. A lightbulb went off and I thought...*Hey! I can tell stories!*

I know what your inner critic is saying: "But I'm terrible at telling stories!" "I have no imagination." "I'm not creative."

Do you like to gossip? Then you're a storyteller.

Do you watch TV shows and movies? Then you know what role characters play in a story.

Do you play video games? Then you understand what a plot is.

Where Do You Start?

Where do you start? You start with what you know. Hook students with something interesting that has happened to you or someone you know. Make sure it's school-, age-, and class cohort-appropriate (obviously). You can even tell a story about something you learned that excited you.

For example, one time I was watching videos on my computer and a link came up about people who eat spiders. The screen shot was of an extremely large black spider in the palm of someone's hand. I'm not really scared of spiders. I've held a tarantula before. Let it walk up my arm. Very cool feeling, like little taps along my skin. So delicate. You don't want to get your face too close to one, though, because they'll shoot their hair out into your eyes and that, I imagine, would not feel nice.

Anyway, I stared at the screen with the spider in the hand for a long minute, then scrolled away. Nah, I didn't need to see someone eat a spider.

Then I went back...but did I?

I mean, did I really want to watch people eat tarantulas?

Nope. Definitely not. I scrolled away again, trying to find something else to procrastinate with.

My brain kept going back to it, though. I had questions. Lots of questions. How did one eat a tarantula? Was it still alive when they took a bite? Did they cook it with spices? What did it taste like? Is it crunchy? Probably keto-friendly, right? Would I be able to eat one if I was offered it? Would it be a good idea to know how, just in case?

Actually, yes, I did want to watch a video about eating spiders.

I clicked the link.

The video loaded.

Annnnd I branded my brain with images I will never unsee. Ever. I also confirmed that I'm truly fascinated by unconventional things. No judgement. Just curiosity.

I learned a lot about eating spiders and have since gone on to learn about eating scorpions and crickets and grubs, along with all kinds of other worldly delicacies.

Could I bring myself to eat anything like that? Maybe. No, on second thought, I'll think about it some more.

There you go, I just told you a story about curiosity getting the better of me. I didn't go into gory details. I don't know you well enough to determine if you'd be offended by my story so I kept it basic. But I could go into more detail if you really wanted. It's etched into my memory like a tattoo.

Not right now, though. We have work to do.

Voilà! Easy-peasy. In a classroom, if I were to tell that story, you know what would happen next? Questions. A lot of them. Stories about things people have eaten. Community sharing.

You might have questions too or want to share something similar with me, but as I said, we have work to do, so keep reading.

Constructing Stories

- Preplan your stories as much as you can. Off-the-cuff stories might be necessary in a pinch but it's better for you and your students if you think up the story or stories you tell a particular class. You need to know enough about your students to know what might work for them, but that's difficult in the first few days of getting to know them. Go with something you've recently learned or experienced. Maybe you went to a summer fair and tried a hamburger stuffed between two donuts. Or maybe you drove all day to take your kids to a giant jumpy castle that was two soccer fields in size, then ended up finding out that adults were allowed inside too. (*There is a traveling gigantic inflatable obstacle course in Canada that you can go to, with kids or without. If that excites you, you should do an internet search right now.)

- Storytelling builds community: A story about something I learned or experienced is a story that students can build on. After telling a story, I turn to the students to share something they've learned or experienced, then, if it's part of my lesson plan, I turn them to a writing activity or creating a storyboard, or some outlet for them to share their own stories. It's a get-to-know-you activity that can turn into a curriculum activity. This would be a low-stakes way for me to introduce students to storytelling, modeling storytelling, then giving them a chance to talk about themselves in some informal way. I would then build on that by teaching concepts of storytelling and writing, as well as something about whatever subject we're covering. Maybe we're learning about metamorphosis and I tell a story about a frog that I raised from tadpole, then students share what they know about transformation. We then continue to learn and continue to tell stories about what we're learning.
- A good story can charm a class: The class I described above was my very first real experience in teaching. I had thirty-six students in a room that could hold twenty-five. Desks were on top of desks. There was no room to move. Energy was high and pulsing. This cohort had traveled together for two years without being broken up. They knew how to push each other's buttons. I was brand-new and so very in over my head.

Please keep this in mind when I tell you what story I chose to hook them with.

Fall 2004

I walk into class, determined to win these students over, an idea fresh in my mind, one I think just might work to capture their attention. They stream in hot, ready to poke and rile one another. I do my best to get them settled, waiting patiently while they slide nosily into their seats, then I take a deep breath, let it out, and start talking.

"I need to tell you all what happened at my house last night," I say with a sigh as I slump down on my desk as if I'm too exhausted to stand.

Insert snickers and a few jokes that I ignore.

"I was walking by the kitchen on the way to let the dog outside and I noticed something strange." I pause, shaking my head. "I swear I closed all the cabinets when I was done in there earlier but when I walked through there were three cabinet doors wide open and I'm alone in the house, right? My husband works nights so it's just me and Kasha, my dog. I know I closed those cabinets."

I shake my head, peeking at my class.

Suddenly, all eyes are on me. I feel the students taking interest. They aren't on the hook yet but they're nibbling on the worm. The fidgeting has stopped. So have the whispers.

"So I go to let my dog out. I'm gone for maybe two minutes." I pause. No one is talking. No one is squirming. "When I walk back into the kitchen there are four cabinets open."

One student at the front gives a full body shiver. Another one puts his hand up.

"Your house is haunted," he says with authority. "That's what ghosts do. They mess with your stuff. It might be a poltergeist. They like to mess with things."

And that, my friends, is how I tamed the wildest class I've ever experienced. Was telling a ghost story my best, most professional moment of my career? Nope. Did I take a huge risk in possibility scaring students and or triggering some? Yep. Did I know any better? Absolutely not.

But it worked.

It worked so well that I told another story the next day, then the next. All the while spinning this lore that my house, which is old as dirt, was haunted. Every day, students would show up early to find out if something else had happened in my house. Every day, I was telling new stories. I had no more behavior issues. I had everyone's full attention. Students would come in and share their ghost stories. Students brought me favorite books they loved about ghosts. I learned so much about cultural beliefs and family traditions from all the storytelling. Telling these stories created a bond with my students. We listened to each other and were fascinated by the stories we told.

And this went on for years. I'll admit, it was my crutch for a while as I figured out how to get a handle on classroom management. Did I use it as a bargaining chip? Heck, yes! I'd managed to figure out what students' universal currency was at that period of time and, I'd say, there was a solid three years of telling my original ghost stories to manage classes.

When I decided I needed to phase it out, I found out really quickly that I couldn't. The students wouldn't let me. There was too much demand. Students would negotiate deals with me to get me to tell a story. "Come on, Miss, we'll all hand in our essay a day before the due date if you tell us that story again." It got to the point where siblings, cousins, friends of friends of students would know about my ghost stories and demand I tell them. Students from other classes would show up and demand a story. Teachers wanted to know if my house was haunted and to hear the stories. Students who had graduated years before whom I bumped into while out and about would ask me for more ghost stories and whether the ones I told had been real. Parents would come in for interview night and want to hear a story.

It was brilliantly successful.

And it was also an overwhelming curse.

Not only was it really hard to come up with new stories all the time but I was tired of telling the same stories repeatedly and I lost track of all the ones I'd told so students would call me out on any deviations.

It took a little while but I finally got rid of the ghost story reputation. I do still occasionally have someone ask about them, but I'm no longer being bombarded with, "Just one more" story requests.

I feel that, in my desperation, I'd snatched at something that was compelling enough to hook my students and, despite it being risky as a subject, and not something I would do now with our current crops of students, I learned just how valuable storytelling is as a tool.

Storytelling, the Tool

- Teach through storytelling: This is easier than pulling a story out of thin air because teaching through storytelling is about using things that really happened to enhance the lesson you're teaching. No matter what the subject is, if you can find a story to tell that relates to the subject matter of your lesson, the information will be more engaging and digestible for students.

It also helps the information stick. Think about it: our ancestors used storytelling to teach lessons, pass down information, and explain things in their world. It doesn't matter what age or grade you're teaching, either; a good story transcends age. Students love to be read to as well no matter the age so even if you don't memorize a story about how a star is made, you can find a story about it and read it to students. I swear to you, even seventeen-year-olds like to be read to.

- I like to encourage students to use their creativity to teach one another things through stories. *Can you think of a time when... Tell your partner about something you saw on our nature walk yesterday...*
- If a student shows me something to get a reaction, I get a story out of them. For example, while supply-teaching during the pandemic, I was in a class where the students all had computers and work to do. I, as I normally do, circulated through the room, checked in with everyone causally, making sure they understood that I wanted them working. I came upon a student who was watching a video of a hunter butchering a deer for food. Now, did I suspect this student was watching this to get a reaction out of me? You betcha! He'd been late to class and slow to get his computer out. He had been angsty about telling me his name for attendance and overall had an edge to him. I'm pretty sure he was expecting me to freak out over the video. Instead, I asked if I could watch too, then pulled up a chair and leaned in to see better. "This is fascinating!" I said. Then I started asking questions. "Do you hunt?" "Have you ever tried deer meat?" "Is it tasty?" "Do you think you'd be able to butcher like that?" Etc, etc. Showing an interest in what he was watching brought life into this student. He straightened from a slouch. He pointed things out in the video and he taught me things about himself, his family traditions, and hunting. Even when I got up to check in with the other students and came back to him, a bond had already begun to form so he told me another story about something he'd experienced. Being open rather than reactionary to something that might seem inappropriate or off task at first glance invites conversation and through conversation you learn things about students. Showing curiosity with no judgement allows for trust to build. I went to that school a few times and when I ran into that student in the hall, he'd stop and chat with me. Relationship built. *Check.*

The thing about storytelling is that it can lead to intimacy in ways that might make you vulnerable so I'd like to end this chapter with a few cautions.

- Put your teacher hat on before you tell a story — something I failed to do when I was a newbie teacher. Make sure your story isn't going to trigger or upset students.
- Don't share too much about yourself. You want to maintain a boundary with students so they don't think of you as a friend. Telling a story about a fun time you had at a fair is fine. Telling a story about how drunk you got in grade 7 at a fair is not fine.
- If you don't know any stories, or aren't comfortable telling made-up stories yet, bring some to read. As I said earlier, students, no matter the age, love to be read to. You could bring in an interesting article or even tell them about a podcast or show you really liked.

- Remind students that if they tell you a story — even if they say it's made up — that involves hurting themselves, hurting others, or being hurt, you have a duty to report it.
- Be prepared for that to happen. It comes with the territory of storytelling and building trust: A student, at some point, will share a story that you'll have to take action on immediately. It might be something they say that's oppressive or inappropriate. They might share something that needs the involvement of Admin and/or parents/guardians. They might tell a story that requires child services to be called. You've done nothing wrong if this happens. It comes with the territory of building community. It usually means that a student feels safe enough to share. You need to act appropriately to get the child help or to help the child learn.

You might consider storytelling to be a next-level skill. Maybe it is. It's not something that comes easily for everyone but we all have experience with storytelling in some capacity. It's built into our primordial genes and has been passed from generation to generation in a variety of ways. With practice, it's something that has impact on building community in our classrooms, but, like the next step, it takes a certain kind of dedication and daily reflection to tease out what works, what doesn't work, and what we're comfortable with.

In Short

- Storytelling is not a waste of time, it's a legitimate way to build community in a classroom.
- Start with what you know. Hook students with something interesting that has happened to you or someone you know.
- Make sure it's school-, age- and class cohort-appropriate and understand that we have a duty to report anything a student shares that suggests hurting themselves or others.
- Preplan stories with your teacher hat on. You need to know students well enough to know if what you're sharing may be triggering.
- Allow students to share stories too. This isn't just about you telling them something, it's about learning from them and their experiences and knowledge.

STEP 5

Develop Your Classroom Personality

This step, while so vital, is one of the hardest concepts for me to explain. How do you teach someone about developing the "core of their being" into something that will work in the classroom?

Working with What You Have

It's all fine and good if you have a personality that is perfectly suited to being a classroom teacher. Some of us were born to be in the classroom. Many of us were not. I wasn't the kind of person who always wanted to be a teacher. I might have played at being one when I was a kid but school wasn't my favorite place to be, so choosing to spend my entire career in a school was, for a long time, a hard pass.

When I first started thinking about becoming a teacher, a group of university friends sat me down and told me that I would be a terrible teacher. I was too blunt. Too mean. I'd scare the students.

That kept me away from teachers' college for a couple of years until I came to a crossroads and knew it was either teaching or working my way into the publishing industry. I chose teaching. I wanted the summers off to write and I wanted the flexibility to work in the area that I had grown up in because I felt my experience in that region would help me connect with students. Teaching would give those things to me.

It would also give me a chance to become a teacher very much like the one teacher who most influenced me when I was a student. This teacher saw beyond my wild makeup and standoffish attitude and seemed to appreciate that I was good at writing and critical questioning and loved to read. He didn't judge, he inspired, and as a very lost teen struggling with mental health challenges, that changed my educational life. Deep down, I wanted to be that kind of teacher for someone else.

Like most new teachers, I entered teaching as if it were an arena and I was set for battle. I had an arsenal of how-I-was-taught-and-I-survived beliefs. I was in charge. The boss. I was strict. Inflexible. It was my way or the highway. I believed that I had to be tough and a little mean to be a good teacher. To maintain control.

In reality I was scared beyond belief.

It took me about three weeks to realize that the tough approach wasn't going to work. I didn't want students to be scared of me and it was exhausting keeping up a hard-as-nails, standoffish approach when I really did care about the students and what was going on in their lives. For many teachers it takes some time to rid themselves of the strict, tough-love attitude. Some never do. They also never seem to understand why they have such difficult students all the time.

Because, silly, it's not a *them* problem, it's a *you* problem. You don't have bad luck and get all the tough students. You simply get back what you put out.

You get back what you put out.

While I said earlier that most times behavior in a classroom isn't your fault and has nothing to do with you, sometimes, in the cases where teachers are inflexible, judgemental, and unapproachable, it is the teacher's fault.

If your attitude is negative then you're the one causing the problems. It makes everyone wonder why you decide to come to work every day, or why you chose teaching in the first place. If you don't like students and loathe your job, that's what's going to come through to everyone you encounter in your day.

You may have a lot to offer in terms of knowledge and subject expertise but if you can't be kind, then you shouldn't be around students. Your disdain oozes out of you even if you try to cover it up, and students sense it. Many times, classroom management issues arise simply because the teacher doesn't have passion for the work and for the humans who are at the core of the work.

For those of you who really do want to be with students but are terrified of losing control and that's why you're wound so tight, I'm going to offer advice: it's okay to do things differently. It's okay to show compassion. It's okay to be kind. You're not an imposter disguised as a teacher. You won't lose control, not in the way you're most scared of.

I find that it takes about three years for newer teachers to build enough confidence to loosen up. The ones who aren't "born with it" but still want to do what's best for students need some time to find their footing. It also takes about this amount of time for newer teachers to sort out what their student-friendly personality is.

Developing a student-friendly persona is so important.

For classroom management purposes, it is important, mandatory even, that you have a student-friendly personality.

What Is a Student-Friendly Personality?

There are two ways to go about figuring out what your student-friendly personality is. You can work with what you have and use your natural personality to engage students or you can work at creating a persona for your classroom. Both have pros and cons. Both can be easy and hard.

The Natural Way

Are you vivacious, fly by the seat of your pants? More serious and crave sticking to the rules? Do you find humor in almost everything? Have you been told you have a wicked dry wit? Are you sweet and soft-spoken? Loud and ready for fun? Do you talk with your hands? Do you smile a lot? Too much? In a creepy way? Are you sarcastic? Do you tell a lot of dad jokes?

Knowing your personality requires self-reflection and feedback.

In order to use your natural personality in a classroom to your advantage, you need to know your personality. Knowing your personality requires self-reflection and feedback. Usually, we develop our personality as we move through our lives. We enter situations with our personality and often get instant feedback about it. If you're paying attention, people you encounter will let you know a lot of things about your personality simply by their body language and facial expressions. You don't need words to know when you've offended someone; they react instantly and show you with a combination of frowning, flinching, downturning of lips or gaping mouth, flushing of color, etc. Same thing with making someone happy. You don't need words to see that their smile and happy tears all convey that you've brought them joy.

Are you easy to get along with? A push-over? Confrontational? Difficult? An extrovert? Introvert? Does prolonged silence make you itchy? Do you get tangled up in awkward social interactions?

There are many different kinds of personality tests out there that can give you a baseline, but even the shallowest of reflections can give you an idea of what kind of teacher you want to be.

Are you the kind of person who loves a loud, energetic space? Do you crave quiet and smaller crowds?

Do you have patience to wait in long lines or would you rather go, go, go?

Do you like to take your time with things, making sure they're perfect? Do you like to get things done quickly and knock them off your to-do list?

Do you laugh a lot? Are you reserved?

Do you socialize with everyone or keep more to yourself?

Figuring out who you are and how your personality might work in a classroom may be an easy exercise for you. You maybe already have a vision of yourself in a classroom interacting with students. If it's not easy for you, then I would recommend searching online for personality tests and doing some. Figure out what you think to be true about yourself that way.

It's important that we start this journey with some kind of understanding of our real selves, but really, it's the people around us who know what is consistent about us, what our personality patterns are. They are the ones who will help you build a student-friendly personality out of what you already have to work with.

The next way you can come to understand your personality is something you probably have already been doing consciously or unconsciously your whole life, and that is getting facial expression and body language feedback from people you interact with. In order for you to be able to make this data work, you'll need to start paying attention and running some tests. See what happens when you're too nice to someone vs. when you're more reserved. Which one feels right to you? Most comfortable? If you already have suspicions that you might be a little too jokey all the time, then see what happens if you lay off the comedy for a bit. If you're curt with cashiers, try being pleasant, test your comfort level out, see what feedback you get. We aren't going to do a major overhaul of our personalities; we're going to use the data we collect to help us build onto our natural personality and make it suitable for student interactions.

If you find yourself wondering what your personality is or how you come across to other people, ask them. Tell your friends and family that you're working to define your classroom personality as you develop your classroom-management practice. I bet they'll be willing to help you figure out what about your personality will work in a classroom and what won't. Frankly, I think it's good practice to ask for feedback anyway, even if you think you know yourself pretty well. You might be surprised by what you learn.

One thing to keep in mind, though. You need to make sure you ask people who know the current version of your personality. Not someone who knew you twenty years ago and you haven't talked to in ten. You need current feedback because our personalities usually evolve all on their own without our intervention and someone who *used* to know you might give you false feedback that won't help.

For example, when I was younger, I was very cranky. My angst was hot and I had extremely high expectations for what I considered common sense. It wouldn't be unusual for me to get snappy with a waiter who didn't get my order right or a cashier who asked me something I considered pointless conversation. I was unpleasant, obviously dealing with my own issues, and I took it out on people around me.

In the twenty-five years since then, I've grown. I've made peace with my angst and the hurt that fueled it. I've atoned for my mistakes and forgiven myself for the way I used to be. I've grown and changed and now approach things in a mature, socially acceptable, and pleasant way. However, I have a friend who knew me back then and when I go out for dinner with her, she preemptively warns me not to be a jerk to the waiter. It's the first thing she says: "Angie, be cool, don't snap at the waiter." She can't see, no matter how many times we've gone out to eat, that I'm not like that any more and haven't been for a very long time.

Would I ask her for feedback about my current personality? Nope. She's stuck in the past and I need to know what's working or not working for me right now.

Some very brave teachers ask their students for feedback about their teaching style, classroom expectations, and their overall enjoyment of the learning, with a survey at the end of a term or school year. When you ask students for feedback, you're going to *get* feedback. If, and only if, you make it safe. Which means you'll need to make sure it's anonymous or you probably won't get any honest feedback.

Sometimes it's just a matter of listening throughout the time you have students. They might tell you that you're silly or a lot of fun. They might show you with facial expressions and body language how they feel you're doing. If a student slumps when you walk up to them, then they probably aren't looking forward to what you're going to say or are readying themselves for something negative. Or they know you're going to end whatever fun they *were* having. If the whole class shoots their hands up to participate, then you know you've created a space that makes them want to contribute, which probably means you're doing a good job at being student-friendly.

You're not going to be able to control what kind of feedback you'll get, so doing this work means developing a thick skin. Not so thick that you don't take the feedback and use it but thick enough that you don't feel crushed by what you learn. Because you'll probably learn things you don't like. It takes incredible vulnerability to open yourself up to feedback from students or from anyone, especially about something so personal.

I think it's worth it, though, because understanding your personality is key to making classroom management work.

Core Traits for Every Classroom

There are some core traits that I believe need to be developed as a "personality foundation" in order to win at classroom management.

- Flexibility: you need to bend but not break. You need to be open to the ideas of others, especially your students. You need to prepare yourself for change and be okay with it.
- A sense of humor: even better, the ability to laugh at yourself. Be humble in that you are not above laughing at yourself for doing something silly. This is also connected to being flexible when things don't go according to plan. If you're a jokester then you need to be prepared to get back what you send out. You'll need to be okay with being the butt of a joke sometimes. Don't take it personally and get offended. Laugh with your students.
- Sincerity: be genuine and kind and, at times, show your humility. You are not above anyone else in the space you occupy and as a human you are fallible. Be okay with that. A little vulnerability goes a long way in creating a safe environment.

There is some danger of crossing boundaries when you're too jokey. Tread carefully so you're not stepping over the line and becoming a "pal".

I had a rowdy class one year with a student I'll call David. I'd been warned that David was "extremely difficult". I'd heard some horror stories from his past teachers and suspected that he would be a challenge, a.k.a a wild card.

As we settled in over the first few days and started opening activities, David fell into similar patterns of behavior that seemed to be his norm. He talked while I taught, laughed loudly at odd times, refused to complete work in class or for homework. It was a lot for the first week of school. That was his thing, though, true to the warnings I'd received, David was difficult.

At least he was predictable. His behavior didn't waver each day.

He expected me to react in a way that he was used to. I wasn't sure what that was; I don't tend to do things the way other people do so I reacted the way that I thought he needed. I ignored most of his outbursts, waited him out if he was speaking over me, spoke to him quietly and offside when I absolutely needed to and didn't take things personally.

Then one day, I came to work really frazzled. I'd left my coffee on the roof of my car and had lost it to the sidewalk. I'd gotten stuck in traffic so I was later than usual arriving at work. I was uncaffeinated and in no mood for hiccups. While teaching my lesson, David made a few sarcastic comments in an attempt to derail me and I called him out. Loudly. Publicly. Sarcastically and, probably the worst, called him by the wrong name.

Not my best moment.

Insert awkward silence. Everyone was shocked. This was completely out of character for me. David was glaring, clearly ready to bolt from my class, never to return.

I was mortified.

I abandoned what I was doing, which got the full attention of the class, walked to him, and apologized sincerely for getting his name wrong, for raising my voice, and for being sarcastic.

In front of his friends and classmates.

I didn't make excuses.

He nodded. Said it was okay.

I knew it wasn't.

That moment was pivotal. It changed everything between us. He later told me that he'd been yelled at many times by teachers but not one teacher had ever apologized to him and meant it.

Down the road, he gave me a gift from his personal stockpile of Disney collectibles, knowing I loved a certain skeleton figure. I cherish it still. It sits on my desk and reminds me every day about the power of humility and the impact I wield in students' lives.

- Willingness to listen: open ears, full attention, absorbing what another person is saying. You might not love what you're hearing. You might feel the urge to argue. Tamp it down so you can actually notice not only the words but the facial expressions and body language. I promise you, it will help you to bond with students if you're actually taking in what they're saying.
- Compassion: show your concern, even if you can't put yourself in the student's shoes or see it from their perspective. Be helpful — remove roadblocks, be an advocate, do something that eases each student's stress and pain.
- Empathy: this is the most important foundational element of a student-friendly personality. It's really hard for some people to grasp because it requires that you put yourself in another person's shoes, not only to see but to understand their perspective and feel some level of what they are feeling. It's beyond sympathy in that you aren't just feeling sorry for something someone is going through, you're able to know or imagine what it feels like and feel it with them.

Often empathy is only possible once you've had a similar experience to that of a student. It's incredibly difficult to empathize about something you haven't personally gone through. I find that this is where a lot of classroom management strategies fall short.

When I first started teaching, I had a very tough attitude about getting work done, presenting things in front of the class, being prepared for tests — all the traditional beliefs that I had been forced to endure as a student (which, I might add, hadn't worked well for me). For some reason, maybe because I didn't know what I was getting myself into as a teacher, I expected my students to push through, suck it up, and just do it.

Anxiety started entering my sphere as a teacher with students who were being "accommodated" from having to make public presentations or write tests; some were even exempted from meeting deadlines. I had a very hard time accepting this accommodation. I pushed back. Made it difficult for students to back out of doing what I felt was going to better prepare them for life. After all, I had been forced to do these things and look at what I'd accomplished.

As adults, we can't judge students by standards we had time, training, and education to rise to.

Then, about seven years into my career, I started feeling extremely overwhelmed by workload and work/life balance. I pushed myself to be stellar at my job, to work through whatever discomfort I was feeling even though my health began to be impacted. I would experience racing heart and palpitations as I was trying to go to sleep, mind racing, loss of appetite, severe headaches and I never made the connection to my own role in those symptoms.

I reached a breaking point when I landed in the ER with blood pressure so high that the ER doctor told me I was a champagne cork ready to pop. He said I was on the verge of a heart attack or a stroke, maybe both.

Something needed to change.

It was at that time in my life that I realized I was suffering from the effects of anxiety. I didn't want to let anything slip. I wanted to be the best at teaching. The best at marking. I never missed a deadline and I never said no to an ask. Because I was doing that to myself, pushing myself beyond my limits, I also expected my students to do the same.

When I hit my wall, everything changed. I began to reflect on my flawed beliefs and what they had done to me, to the people I interacted with, to my students. It was at this point that I developed empathy for students with anxiety. I knew how it felt, I'd just never identified it as anxiety. I always thought it was stress and stress was something I thought I could control.

Well, I controlled it so well that I almost had a heart attack. Talk about a giant fail.

From that experience, I finally understood what it meant when a student told me about their anxiety. Not only that, but I was able to empathize with other things students were going through. Why? Because I started reflecting on my own experiences and began making connections to other people.

With practice, and time, I got to the point where I could empathize with students about things I'd never personally experienced. I was able to do this because I put their well-being at the forefront of everything I did. Being able to put yourself in someone else's shoes doesn't take a lot of imagination; we've all experienced a range of emotions due to loss, stress, disappointment, helplessness, happiness, and excitement. Being able to empathize means you can take those familiar emotions and apply them to something someone else is going through, then feel it with them.

Without empathy, there is no care, and without care, there is no ability to give students what they need and what benefits their overall emotional wellness.

Without empathy, there is no care, and without care, there is no ability to give students what they need and what benefits their overall emotional wellness.

The list of personality traits I've given you in this chapter are base-level, your foundation. You need these characteristics, in some form, to build your personality. They are characteristics, I think, we could all benefit from as humans. You don't have to have an all-encompassing grasp of these things but you have to have some kind of grasp.

What I mean is that you might not have a conventional sense of humor, or clown around constantly, but you laugh at some things, right? You do find some things funny, I'd imagine. You might not love bending to someone else's will but you'll grin and bear it sometimes, won't you? You might not always understand why someone is upset but you can sympathize to some degree, right? Sympathy can be a gateway to empathy if you open yourself to it. We're not talking of extremes here, it's certainly not black or white. There are degrees and variations of everything to do with personality.

Above and beyond these six foundational elements of classroom-friendly personality is what makes you unique as a person.

Time to Reflect

Once you have gathered data from outside of yourself, you need to do some reflecting. Reflecting means that you examine the evidence you've gathered and determine if these aspects of your personality are ones that work in a classroom or that don't work.

This is going to be hard. A lot of people don't know how to take criticism and apply it to make change because it's difficult to examine parts of ourselves that other people think are flaws. And worse, it's not something that happens and it's over. Once you learn how to reflect, you'll start to reflect about everything. All the time. Which is good, but it also can send you into a spiral of self-loathing that is hard to get out of.

I have always been a very sensitive person and, when I was younger, my self-esteem was not healthy. I had grown up with an undiagnosed learning disability, accommodations weren't common practice, and I had a family member who constantly told me how stupid I was. My parents pushed me to believe that I could achieve anything if I worked hard enough but I didn't always understand what I was doing, hit roadblocks in understanding, and got frustrated by failures that kept piling up. Luckily, I've always been tenacious and strove, out of spite, to achieve the things that I was expected to achieve. I somehow came out of it with both positive and negative coping and learning mechanisms and a really, really big chip on my shoulder.

When I began my self-reflecting learning journey, I soon realized that my school experience helped me in the classroom. My bad experiences, the coping mechanisms I'd developed, could make me a better teacher but not if I imposed the same bad strategies that were used with me on my students. My experience would help me because I could empathize with students who felt as I had felt — unheard, misunderstood, invisible — and I could empathize with students who were driven to achieve, who wanted to make someone proud. I could help them learn how to make themselves proud, to feel and be driven by internal validation.

Strategy: How to Reflect

After you solicit feedback about your personality, however you decide to do it, thank the source. Don't comment. Don't justify. Don't try to explain or argue. Tell them you appreciate their input, then go somewhere you feel safe and comfortable and be alone. Go somewhere you can think.

You might choose to do this all in your head. You might voice-record your thoughts. You might journal or make a mind map. Whatever works for you is what's going to work best.

Recall the feedback that impacted you the most intensely, good or bad. Let the feedback hit you. Sit in the discomfort. Let the emotions the feedback evokes wash over you. Then decide: Is it accurate? Do I keep it or toss it? Does it work for me or not? Does this person's opinion matter a lot or a little? Am I doing harm to others?

And if you're not going to be honest with yourself then skip to the next part of this chapter and save yourself some time. You're not ready for this yet. No judgement. This isn't for everyone.

You might decide to immediately discard some of the feedback but I would caution you about discarding outlier comments just because you only heard them once or twice or because you've gotten feedback that contradicts the outlier. For example, say you get a lot of feedback that you're really funny and your jokes make your classroom exciting. You get one comment that your jokes go too far sometimes and you hurt feelings but don't seem to care. Rather than discarding this outlier because you have more data to disprove its validity, you should reflect on the possibility that both things can be true at the same time. Your jokes can make a classroom fun for most students but there are times when your jokes go too far and you might be hurting someone just to get a laugh.

Being aware that someone thinks your jokes are sometimes mean should help you reflect in the moment. It's not meant to make you paranoid or dampen what makes you a favorite teacher to most students. You can still be funny and tell your jokes, but you can also build in a moment of reflection and ask yourself, Is this joke going too far? Did I just say something that might hurt a particular person? If the answer is yes, then change course, tell the joke in a slightly different way or kill the joke and deliver a new one. If the words come out and you realize that you've hurt someone, even if it's days later and someone else had to tell you, apologize.

Being reflective isn't meant to cramp your style or make more work for you. We can bring our unique personalities into the classroom as long as we place them on top of the six foundational aspects I talked about earlier. Ultimately, what makes us unique and engaging as people will be interesting to students but can't be let loose at work, in a professional setting, without some checks and balances. We do have expectations, standards, of professionalism that we need to remember and abide by.

So, whether you're super into pranks, or a rule-follower, or a clean-o-holic, or an absolute geek for something or you like quiet and serenity, or chaos, you must be able to check yourself to make sure you haven't imposed any of that blindly on your classroom to the extent that you are causing discomfort or even harm to your students.

We should absolutely bring our outside personality into the classroom.

We should absolutely bring our outside personality into the classroom. The things that make us unique, our interests, our experiences, our beliefs, our passions, can make a learning environment engaging but we must do it with care and consideration.

Sometimes I'm in a mood that brings out the worst in my personality. Something sets me off and I'm snappy and, at times, growly. Rather than doubling down on those traits, taking it out on everyone around me, and because I'm used to reflecting, and I listen to the people I work with (who have no issues telling me when I'm being unpleasant), I know when it's time for a reset. A reset for me is going for a walk on my lunch hour. Giving myself time to think. Time to step away from whatever it is that's setting me off. I know you've probably heard that exercise can be a wonderful reset for mental health struggles. What it really does is break the pattern of my negative mood by giving me something else to focus on, thereby allowing me to move on. The brisk air, the pounding of my heart, the podcast I'm listening to, it all helps to reset my attitude. I know there's science behind it all, but what I'm telling you is that I've experienced the benefits first-hand every single time.

That's how I manage, how I use reflection on a daily basis. I notice when I'm being unfair or taking things too far only because I pay attention to the impact my words and actions have on others. I don't want to be angry all day or stuck on something that makes me miserable. I don't want to take it out on the people around me. So, I stop. Reflect. Make a change. Move on.

I know what works for me because I've spent years figuring it out. You can figure out what works for you by noticing what your go-to is when you're in a bad mood. How do you change your attitude? If you don't have a healthy way to do that, I recommend spending some time figuring that out too. It could be patterned breathing (breathe in for five seconds, hold for five, breathe out for five, repeat). It could be coloring, or singing, dancing, reading, or doing a puzzle. It could be visualizing placing the concern or frustration into a file marked *Deal with later.* Knowing how to defuse ourselves is our responsibility and will go a long way in making our personalities palatable to our students.

You need to own all the nuisances of your personality, even if parts of what make you you are unpleasant. Own it all, then decide if you can live with the fact that other people might also think part of your personality is terrible. Consider whether those awful parts of you can be dampened, changed, or hidden when you're with students. Developing a healthy, realistic self-esteem will convey confidence. Owning what you can live with is as crucial as reflecting on what you want to change.

It's essential to understand, of course, that interacting with other personalities, at times, might lead to clashes. As the professional that you are, you may need to adjust if your personality doesn't suit a student's personality. Don't turn it into a competition of whose personality will win; back down and meet the student where they are. For example, if you are big into friendly pranks but you have a student who finds pranks to be unfair and hurtful, then you have an obligation to set aside the pranks. Don't prank that student, especially not to prove to them that it's funny and fun. Just don't. It might inhibit you because you have to suspend something that is fundamental to who you are, but for the sake of the student's comfort and safety, you must swallow it.

Understand that this kind of reflective work takes time. It takes trial and error. It takes honesty with oneself. It will mean growing, learning, accepting and committing to change, working through shame and ego, and coming out with a new understanding of yourself.

I may be asking too much of you right now. I may be pushing you too hard to dig deep at a time when you are vulnerable and unable to do the work. And doing this work, opening yourself up to students in these ways, does make you more vulnerable and can become overwhelming.

So, if this is you, completely overwhelmed by what I've just covered, I have another option.

Developing Your Student-Friendly Personality/Persona

I'm a big believer in the concept of fake-it-till-you-make-it. If you can't get your natural personality to fit with the classroom then you're going to need to create a persona that fits. This persona might be a huge departure from your natural state. It might be the mask you wear to keep yourself from being someone you don't want to be while at work or it could be a thin veil that hides a few little quirks that won't work with students.

For example, I have always been very pessimistic. Pessimism doesn't fly well in teaching. It's a downer. A mood killer. So, I work very hard to be customer-service pleasant, medium-sized upbeat, looking on the positive side, mostly, and because being negative (realistic) is very natural for me, I use humor to temper it. I let a lot of things go that normally would stick to me and make me itch. It's not easy. It's exhausting at times, but that's what I do to make myself more palatable in my work environment. If I'm getting too negative, I go for a walk.

Of course, the same foundational pieces apply as when developing your natural personality. If you work with students, you need to also work on: being flexible, having a sense of humor, being sincere, actively listening, being compassionate, and feeling empathy.

The key to creating a persona that works with students is tapping into something you're passionate about. Same principles apply: you're going to need to reflect on what you love, what revs your engine, and whether or not your passion will be appropriate for the classroom.

Let's do the work:

- What do you like spending your time doing?
- Are you fanatical about something? Do you go to every comic convention you can? Are you a movie buff? Do you love cats? Are you into comedy?
- What is your passion? Do you love gardening? Do you get excited when you talk about a certain educational subject: Reading? Robotics? Math? Or general subject: Gems? Green energy? *Star Wars*? Are you a foodie? Do you love apparel? Architecture? Engineering? Purses?
- Is your passion, your favorite thing in the world, the way you spend your time, appropriate to bring into the classroom? Could it trigger students? Can you talk about it in front of parents? The principal? Other teachers?

I'm going to pause here to add a caution. No matter what your passion is, no matter how much you love it and think others should too, no matter how excited you are about whatever it is, you must bring it into the classroom in a tempered way. Developing a persona that is constructed, in part, by the thing(s) you love can lead to imposing your passion(s) on students, which can be overwhelming and silence them.

Let me give you an example. I worked with a teacher for a time who was obsessed with science. On the surface of things that's not a bad thing, right? Scientific study applies to the world around us every day. Inquiry approaches, experimentation, trial and error can all be good things. Talking about subjects in the context of science, like nature and recycling, natural disasters and endangered species, is definitely constructive. But doing this at the expense of student voice and choice is a problem. When a student brought in a book to read that didn't have to do with science, they were scolded and told not to bring it again — scientific material only. If a student submitted work that wasn't formatted as a scientific lab report, there were mark deductions. While this teacher was very enthusiastic and engaging when it came to teaching anything that could be spun in a scientific way, things that couldn't were taught with less enthusiasm.

So, if you're the type of passionate person who can't get enough of birds, *Star Trek*, monsters, squirrels, etc, and you want to bring that love into the classroom not only to share with students but because it makes teaching exciting for you and also makes you an exciting teacher, please do. Please do it in a way that allows students to express and/or discover their passions and honors their voices. Understand that if all of your lesson plans have a theme showcasing the same character, images, gifs, it'll get old, maybe not fast but eventually. While it's fun and cool that students know you love all things Disney, it's important to highlight diversity in all the ways you can.

Once you know what you're going to create as your primary school-appropriate persona, you need to work on how to incorporate that persona into your teaching and learning environment.

- Will you gamify your lessons? Turn learning into a competition of some sort or choose your own adventure-type sequence?
- Will you showcase images, gifs, videos about your passion? How often?

- Will you follow tenets of a particular fandom? Have houses such as Hogwarts? Survival rules à la *Hunger Games*? Music lyrics to live by? Marvel teams? Sport colors or symbols?
- Will you decorate the room to show your passion?
- Will you use language that reflects your passion and label things in a way to immerse students in it as well? For example, I once knew a teacher who was obsessed with the TV show *Friends*. Instead of a reading nook, there was a Central Perk. The craft cabinet was called Monica's closet. A music station was labelled Smelly Cat Corner. So, not only did she introduce her students to the world of *Friends*, which they also seemed to be addicted to, everyone came to understand the allusions that were made in each area of the classroom.
- Will activities be themed to revolve around your interest(s)? Will you give examples in a way that connects to whatever your passion is?

Remember, we're building a persona here because your raw natural personality doesn't quite fit in the classroom or you're not comfortable enough, yet, to bring your natural personality fully to work. That doesn't mean that your persona doesn't embody some of the more palatable aspects of your personality. If you are naturally funny but your jokes tend to run into inappropriate territory, work on being funny in a student-friendly way. We don't want to throw out aspect of ourselves that make us who we are, but we do want to tailor those aspects to fit with who we're interacting with. Don't hold yourself back because you're worried you'll offend someone; instead, reflect on how you can bring those parts of yourself forward in a way that won't offend anyone.

Every day of engaging teaching requires some aspect of theatre. Even on days that you don't feel up to it, you still need to put energy into your interactions.

It's about knowing your audience. And, trust me, no matter how we approach the student-friendly-personality development, we are always being watched and we are, in many ways, putting on a show.

Some days mustering the energy to be enthusiastic for students is very challenging. Sometimes I fail completely at it. I let students know when I'm having a *blah* day. We talk about ways to help one another when we feel like that. Being open about days like that models to students that everyone has off days and that there are ways to make adjustments to help get through those days. You don't want to put your problems on students or vent to them but you can, absolutely, show them how to constructively cope with disappointment and sadness.

"Hey, everyone, I'm feeling a little sad today, why don't we watch some funny videos together for a little while?"

You must account for the age and maturity of your students. Be cautious with your sharing.

I have heard teachers sometimes say, "I'm having a bad day so don't make me mad or you'll regret it." That's a little too honest and not exactly fair. We might be used to taking out our moods on family members but we shouldn't be doing that to our students.

I will let the rowdy group of students who come to the library every day and who I talk to every day about being rowdy know when my patience is wearing thin. We then talk about ways to make everyone happy. It usually works, with a reminder or two, to keep the peace.

Developing a persona allows you to change it up when you encounter different classes as well. If you find yourself struggling with a certain class you might adopt a slightly different persona in order to set a different tone. I think, in many ways, we wear masks in public and around others to help them think of us in a certain way which boosts our confidence and makes certain aspects life more manageable.

On the other hand, wearing a mask to avoid facing part of ourselves that we don't like might cause more harm than spending the time reflecting and doing some deeper work to uncover why we don't like that part of ourselves. The bottom line about creating a persona is that you need to present yourself in a way that works for students. What works for students one year might not work another year in exactly the same way.

Some basic principles:

- Develop an engaging teacher personality that shows your humanity but doesn't cross any lines with students, parents, or colleagues.
- Find a way to express passion for your job — in our work, it's really important that students believe you want to be there, with them, doing what you're doing.
- Be as sincere as you can be, even wearing the mask of your persona. Students are exceptional bull-crap detectors.

What I do know is that our work is too important, too impactful, for us to not put the work into how we present ourselves to students. We must ensure that on a professional level we give students everything they need to be successful, including giving them a fitting attitude.

In Short

- What makes us unique and engaging as people will be interesting to students. We are, however, in a professional setting and need some checks and balances to ensure we're not triggering or offending anyone.
- If you work with students, you need to also work on: being flexible, having a sense of humor, being sincere, actively listening, being compassionate, and feeling empathy.
- For classroom-management purposes, it is important, mandatory even, that you have a student-friendly personality.
- Develop an engaging teacher personality that shows your humanity but doesn't cross any lines with students, parents, or colleagues.
- Find a way to express passion for your job — in teaching, it's really important that students believe you want to be there, with them, doing what you're doing.
- Be as sincere as you can be, even wearing a mask or persona. Students are exceptional bull-crap detectors.
- You may have a lot to offer in terms of knowledge and subject expertise but if you can't be kind then you shouldn't be around students.

Template: Creating Your Student-Friendly Persona

Use this reflection template to help outline your natural personality traits and passions and to hone or create a student-friendly persona.

Reflection

1. Traits and Passions

- What are your core personality traits (e.g., patient, energetic, creative)?
- What passions or interests inspire you (e.g., movies, outdoor activities, music)?

2. Flexibility

- Think about a time when something unexpected happened. How did you adapt to it?

3. Humor

- What makes you laugh?

4. Compassion and Empathy

- How do you react when someone:
  - tells you something that's bothering them?
  - makes excuses or lies?
  - shares something they're proud of?

5. Listening and Sincerity

- How do you show someone you're listening?
- What are some ways you show someone you mean what you say? How do you convey sincerity?

6. Creating Your Student-Friendly Persona

- What are 5 traits/passions you want to bring into your classroom?
- How will you adapt these traits to be student-friendly?

7. Where Do I Go from Here?

- Make connections between the traits and passions you've identified to your students' well-being and success.
- Choose one or two areas of growth (what parts of your personality don't fit in a classroom but you'd like them to)?

Pembroke Publishers ©2026 *How to Win at Classroom Management in 6 Easy Steps* by Angie Barrett ISBN 978-1-55138-375-0 

STEP 6

Offer Voice, Choice, and Differentiation

I know what you're thinking now: How can voice, choice, and differentiation impact classroom management?

Student-Driven, Responsive Teaching

First let me say that when students feel heard and seen, when they are given the opportunity to drive their learning and choose how to showcase it, they tend to be more engaged in the learning, which usually means they're enjoying what they're doing and/or see value in doing it. If someone is enjoying what they're doing and finds value in it, then what they *aren't* doing is acting out or breaking rules.

Why?

Because behavior issues are a clue that something else is going on. It's not the behavior itself that we need to pay all attention to but the underlying catalyst. If what's going on is that you're force-feeding students work that they find meaningless, or that they don't understand, or that is boring, then of course some are going to act out. Sure, some will comply and get it over with. Some may even enjoy the boring stuff because it's safe and consistent. All you need is one or two disruptive students to hijack the classroom dynamic and if one or two students are disengaged, they'll find better things to do instead, like disrupting the rest of the class.

If you don't believe it, think about your own experiences with mandated professional development at staff meetings. How fulfilling to do you find that kind of force-fed learning? When it's not exciting or interesting to you, it's downright painful.

If you haven't experienced this, you will. Professional development is rarely co-constructed with staff. It also isn't usually delivered in a manner that we, as teachers, are asked to deliver learning to our students. It's typically stale and recycled and has little to no personal connection for us.

Compliance training is the worst because as adults and professionals we know learning about how to use ladders properly and what footwear is appropriate is about safety and therefore important so we should pay attention, but it's also the same information, delivered in the same boring way, every year.

Setting aside the mandatory, yearly health and safety compliance training, I know many teachers wonder why the powers that be don't care about our learning needs, our interests, or our time. Sure, we tend to suck it up and deal with it, but we've had years and years of training/indoctrination in a system that has never really catered to our needs so we're kind of brainwashed into accepting the status quo — it's just the way it is.

"That's just the way it is," by the way, is a terrible mantra for a teacher to stick with if they want to be engaging in the classroom, despite what we are put through in our professional training. Other fall-back statements that get my hackles up are, "That's how it's always been done," or, "I had to learn it this way and I survived!"

I'm suggesting doing things differently to make learning more exciting for your students and for you. Our careers typically span at least thirty years, if we can make it to the end. In that time, wouldn't you rather be engaged and not dying of boredom because of what you're doing on a daily basis? I'm not only talking about growing stagnant, but becoming lethargic about the work you're doing so that you can't even pretend to enjoy walking into the classroom.

Our families sometimes don't understand just how much talking we do in a day and the mental and emotional loads we carry or why it causes some of us introverts to crave quiet alone time when we're at home and some of us extroverts to crave adult conversations and socials.

And yes, I know, we get worn down, tired, and burned out with all the things we have to do in this job. It's not easy. It's draining. We're making hundreds of split-second decisions every day, we're dealing with emotional dysregulation in others constantly, we're planning and prepping, marking, calling home and talking…so much talking. It's also really — and I mean crucially — important work.

At one point in time, I'm hoping, you were really excited about teaching, honored to have been given the role of caring for and helping students grow into their future plans.

I can't help you with the burnout other than by telling you that it took me at least fifteen years to figure out a work/life balance that made things easier for me so I could reconnect with my love for my work once again. I hope it doesn't take you that long. I'll tell you my secret, though: I stopped saying yes to everything. I stopped marking over the holiday breaks. I started using my sick days rather than toughing it out. It wasn't easy. I've already told you about my perfectionism and need to be the best, but my body and brain were worn out and I hated coming to work every day so something had to change.

I made myself a priority. Took time to rest and heal. I became a nicer person because I wasn't as stressed out constantly.

I don't know what will work for you but if you're hating work every single day and could care less about engaging your students and that makes you feel guilty, you're probably in survival mode and something needs to change.

What I also know is if you stick to the same stuff every year, you're going to get bored. Being bored might make you irritable, it might make you restless, and it definitely will make you boring.

Think about this from the perspectives of students who are in the system, typically, for twelve-plus years. Twelve boring, predicable, repetitive years. How many times do students "learn" about speeches, do you think? My own kids learned it every year while they were in elementary and yet they still never learned how to write an *engaging* speech for a purpose and a specific audience. There was no continuum at their school, no progression of speech development, just, "This is the unit on speeches" — the same thing every year: "We're going to watch some famous speeches, pull some words together, then end everything with a speech contest." It's not just speeches either. I can't count the number of birdfeeders my kids made. Or how about the working volcano activity that both my kids had to do, four years apart? Same stuff, every year.

I propose doing things differently, shaking up the same old routine, bringing engagement and excitement into the classroom for both you and your students. Please don't freak out! I promise you can do this in a safe and somewhat comfortable way. Baby steps are possible so you can grow into the ideas I'm about to hit you with. It does take some courage. It does ask you to push outside of your norms. I promise you, though, if you stick with me on this, I'll show you how you can prevent classroom management issues with the use of voice, choice and differentiation.

What Do I Mean when I Say Voice?

Students are not empty containers waiting to be filled.

As I've mentioned previously, students don't walk into our classrooms as empty vessels waiting for our wisdom to fill them. They all have their own stories, experiences, heartbreaks, and joys. They also each come into the classroom with a bias about the classroom and school. This is the place where, in theory, they are supposed to be safe and learn things, but many, even at a young age, have learned helplessness, have faced bullying and unfair treatment, and have already given up.

Giving students the opportunity to share their experiences about life and what learning they've already done — at home, at school, at camp, with grandparents, in the garage, at the stream, on a field trip — can open up a lot of information to you about what has been done in the past, what needs there are, what students get excited about, and where their curiosity lies.

Giving students voice allows them to share their interests as well as dislikes and can give them agency to design their own learning. It validates them in ways that inspire engagement, but only if you're willing to listen to them, then to take action so they know they are being heard and their learning needs and desires are being fulfilled.

When you're building your community, doing your get-to-know-you activities, learning what you can about your students, you should also be mining for what they are willing to share regarding their experiences at school. This is not a time for judgement. Even if you are best friends with a teacher who students are telling you didn't teach them how to do a certain element of math the year before, you cannot argue or correct them about it if you want to hold their trust. Also, please don't gossip to your friend about it either; that's a violation, and you know it is. If your students find out, you'll lose them. You must be open to the feedback you're getting. Allow students to tell you anonymously at first so you can get the most honest information possible. Find out what didn't work and what did. Find out what excited them, what the best parts of their school and learning have been so far. Find out what they like to do at home, things they've learned when they're not at school. Honor what they bring you and take action to use it.

While I was home-schooling my son, I discovered that he was very interested in learning how to cook and bake. We incorporated that into his lessons, starting with navigating the grocery store, clipping coupons, paying with cash, understanding credit, working with measurement and temperature, reading and altering recipes, etc. As he got more comfortable, he began experimenting with his own twists on recipes and he branched out to teach himself how to cook different things he liked to eat. I discovered what his currency was, what motivated him to learn, and I designed multidisciplinary lessons to engage him.

I know you might be thinking: but Angie, you did that for one child. How can I do that for thirty-two?

I'm not asking you to write individual lesson plans for every student, not exactly. What I'm asking right now is that you collect information so you can learn what currency motivates the students in front of you. I will show you how you can take that information and give your students' voices a place in your planning.

First, you need to learn about your learners and what they enjoy learning. Find out what they're curious about. Set up a wonder wall or a curiosity corner where students can write down any questions or ideas they have and visit it once a day together to see if there's anything that you can take and run with immediately.

I talked to a teacher who brought pumpkins into his class for decorating at Halloween. One student wanted to know what happened after October 31st. Did the pumpkins just go into the trash or was there something else that could happen? The class researched and learned that pumpkins made great food for wildlife so they took a field trip to the forest behind the school and left pieces of pumpkin in places they had sightlines to.

Every day they went to check out what was happening to the pumpkin pieces. Those little trips spawned learning about ants and how they forage, then to ant colonies and structure, the lives of ants, and the roles they play in a colony. They also learned about how vegetation decays and what that does to the forest floor, how it provides nurturance. They also explored what animals they saw around the pumpkin pieces. They researched squirrels and skunks and birds which all seemed to like eating parts of the pumpkins.

One question about what happens to pumpkins led to so many different learning opportunities. It wasn't planned when it happened but because the teacher was open to it, he found ways to make connections to the curriculum to reflect in his lesson plans because he was open and flexible to pivoting with this exciting learning opportunity. Added to that, because he was able to organize it into a project, at any given time each student was working on something different and bringing their findings to the class to share. Some students were learning about squirrels, some were learning about ants, some were discovering fertilization, but all were meeting the curriculum expectations. Everyone was engaged. Everyone was learning either from their own research or from their classmates. The teacher would do mini-lessons as needed, to help clarify something, to break down a more complicated concept, and/or to teach a skill that students needed on their learning journey. It was a hive of learning and all the teacher had to do was organize a structure so there was a process to the learning and outcomes that fulfilled curriculum expectations.

I'm going to go on a little tangent here, but this topic excites me and has been part of my work with students for many years. It's a huge topic and deserves its own book. In fact, if you want to learn more and take a deep dive into the alternative learning rabbit hole, then you should research the following: Genius Hour, Project-Based Learning, Inquiry Projects, Iterative Learning, and Reciprocal Learning — just to get started.

Even though this teacher didn't start the term with an inquiry project in mind related to pumpkins, because he was open to it and willing to give students the chance to lead their learning, that was what he ended up creating for his students. It's not the most stress-free way of doing this kind of project; in fact, he told me that he felt he was scrambling every day to make it work and the only reason he stuck with it was because he was so engaged himself.

Imagine if you were prepared ahead of time. If you planned for some kind of learning that students decided on and that you supported. I know it sounds like chaos. You might wonder: How will I know what I'm teaching? How will I know what kind of learning students will need? How can I plan for the unknown?

If you start the term with a mindset of project-based learning, scaffold the elements of discovery, idea generation, research, development, testing, trouble-shooting and sharing, as iterations, cycles of learning, then you are open to all the possibilities that students can come up with. Same with inquiry-based learning: if you scaffold the learning so students come to understand what a significant and relevant question looks like, model inquiry for them, use a guided inquiry approach to lead them through inquiry, and get their feet wet (so you have complete control at first), then transition them (when they're ready) to independent inquiry projects, most students will be able to transition seamlessly and run with it. The students who might struggle and need more support will have you there to guide them. It not only gives students agency over their own learning but it gives students at different levels of learning opportunities to help one another and gives you time to help anyone who might be struggling.

This doesn't mean more work for you. Truly, it doesn't. All you have to do is develop a plan that includes the curriculum expectations you want to tackle and an idea of how you want students to achieve the expectations. Say you decide to use project-based learning and you want to use expectations from language arts, science, and math. You set up the project so you know what you'll need to teach as basics so students can grasp what they need to do. You'll need to scaffold learning through the process; some of it you will know ahead of time, some of it will develop as you go. For example, if you know they will be running labs at one point, then you need to teach them how to run a lab safely and successfully. If you plan on grading the end result, the product, then you'll need to teach them how to make whatever the product is; if it's a speech, you'll need to teach them how to write and deliver the speech. Same goes for an essay, or a podcast, etc.

BUT, if you don't plan on grading the essay or the podcast or the speech then you don't have to explicitly teach it. If you're open to what the "product" looks like, if you're more interested in the process and the content and the learning, then you don't have to explicitly teach how to write a speech, essay, podcast, or whatever students dream up to showcase their work. Students will figure that into their project plan and learn about it themselves with no risk of failing if they get it wrong because you're not grading that part, it's just a vessel to hold all their findings and ideas.

I had a student once who wanted to display her learning in the form of a board game. It was an ambitious idea that involved a lot of pieces but would meet the assignment requirements to highlight the curriculum expectations (math and science) that she learned and to teach them to an audience (the game players). She spent so much time crafting game pieces and the board itself. Did her own art and game clue cards. We had a lot of meetings and check-ins to talk about the effort she was putting in. I tried to help her balance the workload of what she'd taken on. I did advise her to pull back what she was doing with the end result because I wasn't grading her on the "product" of the game. I was grading her process all the way through using the assessments I collected. When she ran into a time crunch, we talked about how to achieve her goals without having to sacrifice more time to this elaborate product. I never taught her about making board games, she researched (I assessed research/gave feedback) it as part of her project. She taught me about key elements that needed to be included so that the equations she wanted to teach would work and had conversations with classmates, teaching them along the way (I observed/assessed/gave feedback). She did surveys and research about what went into a fun game (part of her research and communicating findings — assessment/feedback given). We had "think tank" meetings where she got feedback along the way, from me, from her peers, from herself (I assessed), rejigged things, tried again, and overall showcased the iterative process of learning throughout her time working on this project. In the end, she hit the deadline and the game wasn't ready. She thought she'd failed.

I told her that she'd done everything I'd asked her to do — she had already achieved our project goals and met curriculum expectations. I shared with her all the data I'd collected, all the assessments I'd done. We looked at the rubric and I showed her how she had achieved success through the process of her learning.

She insisted on playing her game unfinished with the class. The vital parts were there, the learning with her peers happened. Her grade was high. She was satisfied in some regards but not proud of what she'd accomplished because she hadn't finished the game the way she had envisioned. I assured her that she had done everything I'd asked her to do and advised her to work on the other things she needed to work on. Which she did. But later that year, in the summer actually, I got an email from her with a series of photographs. She had gone on to finish the game and showed herself playing it with a group of friends. This, to me, is the epitome of learning, doing it for the joy and satisfaction of learning, being motivated not by grades but by taking pride in your work. She was finally proud of what she had accomplished and so was I. Several years later, I ran into one of her friends who told me that they still pulled that game out when they got together and had a lot of fun reminiscing. It had a lasting impact.

If you set up project-based learning or some other type of authentic learning experience then you're acting as a facilitator, a guide, and students are the ones driving their learning.

If you set up project-based learning or some other type of authentic learning experience then you're acting as a facilitator, a guide, and students are the ones driving their learning. You will teach them key things and they will teach you key things all while working toward the goal of showing that they are meeting the expectations of the curriculum. This will be done as you have check-ins and conversations. You'll work in checkpoints for feedback and redirection if needed and you'll assess the progress. By using this strategy, you'll realign students who have gone off the rails and you'll correct errors before they become dealbreakers. You'll be able to show how students have worked toward mastering the expectations set out at the beginning of the project and you'll do it in a way that is exciting for everyone because they are doing things that are interesting to them. And, as a bonus, they'll be proud of what they accomplish. If you set it up aiming to lead students into learning key curriculum expectations but keeping it open to their curiosities, you'll find that students are tremendously engaged. If you guide them along the way, using check-ins, conversations, observations, ensuring their success, and building their confidence then you'll find that you're spending far less time grading (especially at the end) and more time investing in your students' success.

"But wait!" You might say. "It can't always be about their interests! There are specific topics and concepts I need to teach them!"

Yes, I know. You're not going to use this type of engagement all the time for every subject. I've seen it done, but let's maybe start small, with baby steps. Even one authentic subject-specific learning experience a term will get your students' engines revving. On top of that you're offering choice in other areas, right? You're giving students more leeway with texts they read/watch/listen to. You'll be giving them some agency over how they use their time. It all adds up to fulfillment and contentment.

How do I know? Because I've done it, I've seen it. Over and over. I've lived it.

How Do You Plan This Kind of Work?

You choose the curriculum expectations you want to cover in the project. For elementary, the expectations can be from different subject areas too! For secondary, you're using the expectations from your subject curriculum BUT my dream has always been to run a cross-discipline project. If you're interested in what that can look like, reach out to me, I have ideas.

You create a marking tool that allows you to track progress. It can be a rubric with curriculum expectations featured somewhere with ranges of what proficiency looks like (i.e., what "learning" looks like) with progress markers along the way and room for feedback/notes. You can grade based on asking critical questions, followed by knowledge acquisition through research, followed by summarizing findings, followed by applying learning to new contexts.

You'll explicitly teach "asking critical questions", "researching", "summary writing", and model what "applying to new contexts" means.

Students will choose what their topic is (you will vet this, of course) and what the end result looks like.

One funny, not-so-funny story: way back in the early days of experimenting with giving students choice, I gave students the option to pick their own speech topics with no parameters other than that it had to be school-appropriate. I only asked that they tell me what their topic was as we started planning. I didn't check in with students throughout the process. We rarely, if ever, had time to work on things in class, that was a practice strictly forbidden and considered "wasted time" by the admin of the time. Students were constructing their speeches on their own time. I was solely interested in the end result and figured my students knew what to do because I'd taught them all the basics of writing and delivering a speech.

A student who was supposed to present his speech the next day asked me to look over his pages to make sure his arguments made sense. As I did, I realized that he was planning on giving a hate speech.

Hard. No.

When he had given me his topic idea, it had been about conformity. My idea of his topic and his idea were vastly different. I told the student that he wouldn't be able to give the speech. He was furious. He called his father and told him that he was going to drop out of school. His father was furious. He came looking for me in the building. Thankfully, another teacher redirected him to the office.

In the end we sorted everything out but it was a pivotal point in my teaching journey. Make no mistake, this was my fault. I should have been checking in all the way through and being diligent about knowing every student's topic ideas from inception to completion. From that point on I always included work time in class for every project so I could have conversations and use observations to ensure that students were on the right track. It was not wasted time. It was meaningful, well used time that I needed to ensure the success of my students.

That being said, I've gone on to have many wonderful experiences with giving choice for various projects.

I've had students write letters to the Minister of Education over curriculum expectations they feel are not suitable to their lives, a.k.a. are boring and meaningless.

I've had students run upcycling campaigns with donated clothes.

I had one student recreate the menu of his mother's restaurant to make it more efficient.

I had a pair of students create a very entertaining magazine about school culture.

I've had various forms of short stories, children's books, crafts, baking, paintings, and clothing design.

All projects may have resulted in different "products" but they showed me that students were successfully learning in the key curriculum areas I was asking them to focus on. And they did it with enthusiasm and so much creativity.

What Is Choice?

Let's dig a little deeper into what I mean when I say choice.

We talked about choice when using discipline for behavior in an earlier chapter. Giving options can free up a standstill and deescalate a situation. It works as long as the choices are limited, easy to meet, and reasonable. Too many choices can be overwhelming.

We're not going for a free-for-all. We need to provide structure and boundaries. We need to scaffold choice so students learn how to navigate more and more freedom to explore their curiosities, and choice needs to be grade- and student-appropriate.

Allowing students to choose what they're working on gives them some room to breathe.

Allowing students to choose what they're working on gives them some room to breathe.

If they're having a slow morning and can't get their brains to tackle math at that moment, giving them the grace to choose to work on something else could help ease them into the day so they are more productive later. Maybe they want to color instead, or read. You don't need to know what, exactly, is bothering the student, but if your gut is telling you that a student needs a different focus, then giving them the choice allows them a sense of control that they may desperately need in that moment. It's a way for them to govern the time they have and it gives you time to work with other students, do check-ins, and keep things low-key.

This can be an established norm in your classroom for the daily start up or it can be something you offer to students who seem dysregulated. There needs to be parameters with choices, like a set time period, so students know there is an expectation to come back to the whole-class activity.

The way I see it, you can give choice in several different areas from work habits to assignments, to assessment/evaluation tasks, to behavioral consequences, to texts they read. Since voice bleeds into choice and choice bleeds into differentiation, I'll get into more examples in a bit.

What Is Differentiation?

Differentiation allows you to cater to the needs of each individual student with regards to activities, assignments, topics, time use, and many other things, and it goes hand in hand with voice and choice. It's like creating an individual education plan for each student without the hard work of creating a detailed education plan for each student. A lot of people think differentiation is next level in terms of workload but it's actually one of the best ways to decrease your workload and do great things with and for your students.

Once you've decided on the curriculum expectations you'll be tackling in a particular unit, then you need to lay out the assessment and evaluation expectations: the goalposts you'll be asking students to aim for.

As I mentioned earlier, you can create one grading schema, a master rubric if you will, and put expectations into it, swapping the different expectations each time you use it. Add some kind of scale to show learning, then voilà! You've cut your workload down and given yourself so much freedom in creating engaging assignments.

Here are samples of a grading grid and a template for student reflection I put together.

Obviously, this is very basic, but you get to decide what elements you want in your master rubric.

Following is a brief template for students to reflect on their learning.

Template: Grading Grid

Assignment Name: ______________________________

Student Name: ______________________________

Date: ______________________________

Curriculum Expectations & Proficiency Scale

Curriculum Expectations	Proficiency Level	Comments (specific feedback/observations/ conversations)

***Proficiency Level Key: (Use adjectives to describe what you want students to be able to show you based on the curriculum expectations you've taught them.) *Note: It doesn't have to be 4 levels! It can be a sliding scale, a bull's-eye, or some other method you want to show students how they're progressing.**

Level	Description
4	**Excellence** — deep understanding/expertise; applies concepts creatively and independently
3	**Approaching Excellence** — consistent and accurate understanding and application of concepts
2	**On the Border of Excellence** — partial understanding; some forward momentum and a lot of potential

Pembroke Publishers ©2026 *How to Win at Classroom Management in 6 Easy Steps* by Angie Barrett ISBN 978-1-55138-375-0

Level	Description
1	**At the Outskirts of Excellence** — limited understanding; minimal forward momentum, potential may be temporarily stuck
N/A	Not assessed at this time

Overall Notes / Observations / Next Steps

Pembroke Publishers ©2026 *How to Win at Classroom Management in 6 Easy Steps* by Angie Barrett ISBN 978-1-55138-375-0

Template: Student Reflection

What did you do well on in this assignment/unit?

____

____

____

What did you struggle with or what might you still need to work on?

____

____

____

List two goals for the next assignment or unit.

1. ______________________________________

2. ______________________________________

List three steps you'll take to improve your learning outcomes in the next assignment/unit.

1. ______________________________________

2. ______________________________________

3. ______________________________________

Pembroke Publishers ©2026 *How to Win at Classroom Management in 6 Easy Steps* by Angie Barrett ISBN 978-1-55138-375-0

Now that you have chosen the curriculum expectations and you know that you'll be assessing through the process and that the data you collect will ultimately inform your final evaluation of the project as a whole, you can figure out how you'll facilitate the process.

Never forget that you must explicitly teach anything you're grading.

Which elements need to be explicitly taught to ensure students' success?

When will scheduled check-ins occur? What will they look like?

How will you chunk (create a step-by-step process) this task so it's manageable?

What samples will you use to show students examples of what the steps in the project look like? I know some teachers who actually do each step with students and create a model for students to see as they're working. Have students critique models so they can learn what works and what doesn't work with different kinds of projects.

How and when will you give feedback? Tell students as they are working if something is on track or not. Don't keep secrets from them. You know what you're looking for; tell them.

When I've talked about this with teachers who are sceptics, I've gotten some scoffs, some incredulous stares, some downright full stops.

Change can be scary, I know! But offering voice, choice, and differentiation works.

Here's a lesson plan to show how to include voice, choice, and differentiation using the Ontario Curriculum.

Sample: Grade 7 Science Lesson Plan with Voice, Choice, and Differentiation

Topic: Human Impact on Ecosystems
Strand: Life Systems
Time: 60 minutes approx. (You can adapt this to stretch into multiple days.)
Big Question: How do human activities have both a positive and a negative effect on ecosystems?

Curriculum Connections (Ontario)

Overall Expectation

- **B1.** Assess the impact of human activities and technologies on ecosystems and evaluate ways of minimizing negative impacts.

Specific Expectations

- **B1.1** Assess the effectiveness of various actions that support the sustainability of ecosystems.
- **B2.2** Analyze interactions within ecosystems, including the impact of human activity.

Learning Goals (Shared with Students)

- We will explain how humans impact ecosystems.
- We will explore solutions that reduce negative environmental impacts.
- We will choose how we show our understanding.

Success Criteria (Co-Created or Provided)

- I can clearly describe a human activity that impacts an ecosystem.
- I can explain why the impact is positive or negative.
- I can propose one or more solutions or improvements.
- I can share my learning in a way that makes sense to me and others.

Minds On (10 minutes) – *Voice & Curiosity*

Provocation:

"Think about a place in nature that you've visited (a park, lake, forest, beach, trail). How have humans impacted it?"

Options for Engagement (Choice)

- Think–pair–share
- Sketch the place and label changes
- Quick write or voice note

*Teachers: Validate all responses—there are no "wrong" connections.

Pembroke Publishers ©2026 *How to Win at Classroom Management in 6 Easy Steps* by Angie Barrett ISBN 978-1-55138-375-0 

Action (40 minutes) – *Choice-Based Learning Pathways*

Key Learning Activity (Same Big Question, Different Options)
Students explore one human activity and its impact on a specific ecosystem (e.g., littering, air pollution, conversation, farming, etc.)

Student Response Choice (Pick ONE)

Response Action	Product	Who This Helps
Writer	Paragraph, letter, or short article	Students who work well with structure and writing
Designer	Infographic, diagram, or poster	Visual learners
Communicator	Short video, audio recording, or slideshow	Auditory/expressive learners
Investigator	Cause/Effect chart, comparison table	Critical thinkers
Change-maker	Campaign idea, speech, commercial	Doers

Where is the differentiation?

In the Content

- Choice of ecosystem (local or global)
- Teacher-curated resources at varied reading levels
- Optional sentence starters and vocabulary banks

In the Process

- Independent, partner, or small-group work
- Flexible pacing
- Graphic organizers available

In the Product

- Multiple formats
- No single "right" answer
- Focus on understanding, not polish

Teacher Check-Ins

- "Tell me what you're trying to show."
- "What impact do you think is most important?"
- "How could you make your idea clearer?"

*Teachers: Take Observation/Conversation *notes as you do your check-ins.*

Pembroke Publishers ©2026 *How to Win at Classroom Management in 6 Easy Steps* by Angie Barrett ISBN 978-1-55138-375-0 

Consolidation (10 minutes) – *Student Voice*

Choice of Reflection

- Gallery walk with sticky-note feedback
- Exit ticket (written, drawn, or audio):

  "One way human activities have a positive/negative effect on the ecosystem is..."

- Circle share (voluntary)

Practice and Feedback

Assessment Tool: Single-point rubric focusing on:

- Understanding of human impact
- Explanation and reasoning
- Clarity of communication

*Students may **self-assess** or **peer-assess** using success criteria.

Extensions & Equity Considerations

- Invite students to connect to **local Indigenous perspectives** on land stewardship.
- Offer real-world action (school recycling audit, awareness poster).
- Provide assistive tech (speech-to-text, visuals, chunked instructions).

How This Lesson Embodies "VCDC":

Voice → validates lived experiences
Choice → increases engagement
Differentiation → equitable access for all learners
Curriculum-aligned → meets Ontario expectations

Pembroke Publishers ©2026 *How to Win at Classroom Management in 6 Easy Steps* by Angie Barrett ISBN 978-1-55138-375-0

Template: Ecosystems Impact Task — Observation/Conversation Grid

(*You can use a form like this to monitor progress.)

Criteria	**Check-in Date:**	**Check-in Date:**	**Check-in Date:**
Describes a human activity that affects an ecosystem	☐ Demonstrated **Comments:**	☐ Demonstrated **Comments:**	☐ Demonstrated **Comments:**
Explains why the impact is positive or negative	☐ Demonstrated **Comments:**	☐ Demonstrated **Comments:**	☐ Demonstrated **Comments:**
Proposes a realistic solution or improvement	☐ Demonstrated **Comments:**	☐ Demonstrated **Comments:**	☐ Demonstrated **Comments:**
Communicates learning in a way that makes sense to the student	☐ Demonstrated **Comments:**	☐ Demonstrated **Comments:**	☐ Demonstrated **Comments:**

*You can use a self/peer-assessment task throughout the process as a means of check-ins and feedback. Make sure to teach students how to give constructive feedback by assessing with "yes/no/kind of", then offering evidence to support their assessment.

Pembroke Publishers ©2026 *How to Win at Classroom Management in 6 Easy Steps* by Angie Barrett ISBN 978-1-55138-375-0

Template: Self and Peer Assessment

Name: ______________________________

Type: ☐ Self ☐ Peer **Peer Name (if needed):** ______________________________

1. I can clearly describe a human activity that impacts an ecosystem.

☐ Yes ☐ No ☐ Kind of

How do I know?

____

____

2. I can explain why the impact is positive or negative.

☐ Yes ☐ No ☐ Kind of

How do I know?

____

____

3. I can propose one or more solutions or improvements.

☐ Yes ☐ No ☐ Kind of

How do I know?

____

____

4. I can share my learning in a way that makes sense to me and others.

☐ Yes ☐ No ☐ Kind of

How do I know?

____

____

Reflection

One thing done well:

____

____

One thing to improve:

____

____

Pembroke Publishers ©2026 *How to Win at Classroom Management in 6 Easy Steps* by Angie Barrett ISBN 978-1-55138-375-0

Roadblocks to Voice, Choice, and Differentiation

Some teachers don't just throw up speed bumps, like "whoa, slow down," they put up full roadblocks.

Here are a few I've heard:

Pushback: If I tell students what to do to get a great mark, then my marks will be too high. Inflated! Everyone will think I'm going too easy on them.

I'm here to confirm that yes, if you use differentiation and allow for choice and voice in student work, then grades will end up higher. They'll end up higher because students are committed to the work they're doing because it has purpose for them, it excites them, they take pride in it. Your class average will be high because you're ensuring student success by removing all the secrets to success. Why would you want to stop that from happening? What is the rationale to keeping students down? Their success should be your success and if we continue to place a mark value on their work then authentically higher grades should reflect what a wonderful job you're doing facilitating their learning.

Pushback: How will I mark a bunch of different projects?

To streamline this, you'll need to grade how well students learn the curriculum expectations rather than grading them on a particular project. The curriculum doesn't explicitly say, "Students must learn how to create a diorama or a birdhouse." It may give suggestions that name those things but it doesn't say you must leave school knowing how to paint a sunset.

As I've already stated, if you're assessing the process and breaking the task down into steps/chunks, you'll hit curriculum targets that actually show what students are learning, what they need more support on, and what will ensure their success. So, it doesn't matter as much about marking all the different projects, it's more about what learning happened on the journey to the final result.

And honestly, I find it much more appealing to "grade" a bunch of different projects than I do the same essay x 30.

That being said, differentiation can mean that you create opportunities for students to work on different activities with the same goals. Say your goal is for students to learn how to write an essay. You want all students to learn the same components of essay writing; however, you give them an opportunity to choose the type of essay they'll write. Maybe you teach them about persuasive, narrative, and compare/contrast essay writing, then they get to choose which one they will do in this unit. In another unit, they choose a different kind of essay. Or they all write the same kind of essay but they get to choose the topic they'll write about.

Differentiation can mean allowing students to design their own projects that capture the learning goals you've laid out from the curriculum. I will admit, this one in particular is higher-level differentiation and takes some major student-friendly breakdown of the curriculum so they understand the goals. It also requires a lot of teacher facilitation. I usually use this method with "gifted" students who are craving more and who love a challenge.

As long as your focus is on the learning you want to see then differentiation can mean that some students will opt to write a test while others will give a speech and others will create a podcast. This one does mean that you will have the extra step of creating a test but if you're like most teachers I know, you already have a bunch of tests ready to go.

It can mean each student in your class reads a different book! Gasp! Or even not a book, but a magazine, a blog, a car manual or listen to a podcast series or audio book. Yes! It's true, that can be done. Reading is reading after all.

Pushback: But if they all read different things, then how will I know if what they're reading is appropriate? How will I give them chapter questions to make sure they're reading? How will I teach the same theme?

What is or isn't appropriate should be up to the student and the parents/guardians, in my opinion. I'm happy to see students reading anything as long as it isn't promoting hate, so when I give carte blanche choice to students with reading material, I make sure parents/guardians are involved in the process. I explain my rationale for removing censorship from reading selection to students and parents. I teach students about analyzing texts with a critical awareness and how to spot oppression, discrimination, and stereotyping, and what to do about it. I check in with every student frequently and we talk about the material they're reading. I tie work to the reading, not with chapter questions, but with critical thinking questions. What is the background of the author? Whose voice stands out in what you've read so far? Whose voice is missing? Why do you think that is?

I task students with finding themes and making connections to themes from texts their classmates are reading.

I task students with finding themes and making connections to themes from texts their classmates are reading. It's detective work to find the degrees of separation between one text and another. We do this throughout the time that they are reading their different texts and students get really good at finding links and making meaning, forming connections between the material and themes, messages, and new learning. I also use these different reading materials as springboards to inquiry-based projects. For example, as students are reading, they will jot down questions that pop up in their heads, even random ones that don't seem to have anything to do with what they're reading. After they finish reading, we take those questions and tease them out, see if they will lead to a project that inspires discovery or perhaps demands a change in society. Once they settle on the question(s) they want to explore, we start the inquiry project.

It's a really exciting way to make reading relevant and students find it amusing and interesting to hear how one of their peers went from reading a car manual to redesigning the layout of a dashboard for Gen Z drivers to reduce distraction.

Pushback: I won't have as much control. It will be chaos!

You will have as much control as you need or want to have. I promise you, though, if you've planned the unit, the lessons, and the outcomes (assessments and evaluations) then what happens in between is pure magic. Students will teach you things if you're open to it. You'll model how to research on the spot to find answers you need in the moment. You'll overcome obstacles and problem-solve in real time with students. It'll work your brain as well as your students' brains and you'll end your day invigorated and looking forward to what comes next.

I explained earlier how you can design differentiation so that it requires very little work and gives you ultimate control over all aspects of what the students do. In reality, there isn't a part of differentiation that encourages chaos. You will be doing all the planning, you'll know what you need to teach and be able to prep for it. The only surprises you'll encounter will be the ideas your students come up with.

Pushback: How will this prepare students for real life? How will this prepare them for high school or post-secondary?

The most common questions I get from teachers in elementary schools is how to best prepare grade 8 students for high school. Secondary teachers ask me, "How can I ensure my students will be prepared for post-secondary?"

My answer to both is this: you prepare them by teaching them work ethic, critical thinking, flexibility, compassion, and teamwork, and by supporting innovation and creativity.

I don't really think it's our job to prepare students for the next stage of their educational journey as much as it is to teach them how to work respectfully in groups, how to be a part of a team, how to be confident with working independently, how to ask probing questions, how to find credible sources and disseminate information critically. I think it's our job to teach them whatever the curriculum lays out but the method we use to teach them doesn't have to be in one "favored" format. It doesn't have to be via a test or an essay or a particular kind of lab — you can prepare them for life by helping them learn how to be adaptable to any situation, how to problem-solve, and how to innovate.

I'm going to tell you a story about one of the most pivotal moments in my teaching career so far. Consider it a cautionary tale, one that may happen to you at some point, but even if it doesn't, it's worth keeping in the back of your mind when you're making a decision to differentiate or not.

I had a student, whom I'll call Dane, who was a superstar. He completed every project I set out with vigor and to perfection. We talked a lot about why he was doing many of the projects or learning the things I was teaching and I always stressed to him how important it was for him to do things *my way*, exactly as I set them out in my lesson activities, tasks, and assignments. *I knew* what he needed to know for success in his future because I'd been there and done that.

Can you believe my hubris?

It makes me cringe now but, at the time, I did truly believe that I knew, as if I could see into his future, what he would need to be successful, based only on my own experiences in life. So I force-fed him content curated by my belief that I knew what he'd need, even though he didn't even know what he would end up choosing to do once he was finished with school. I demanded he write tests for the "experience" in order to "prepare" for his future. Mind you, I didn't ever actually *teach* him how to prepare for or how to write tests. I tortured him with old, dead, classic literature that he in no way found useful or that connected to his life experience in any way. I chose topics and materials that *I felt* were mandatory for a successful academic life. I did everything all the other teachers were doing by doing what had always been done and I did it with the attitude of "knowing" what was best for my students.

Dane moved on, as students do, and during the many years that came after, I began getting weary of students asking, "Why are we doing this?" all the time. It really started to get to me because I realized my answers to that question were pretty flimsy and I didn't actually believe what I was telling them any more. "We're doing this because we have to so you'll be ready for (insert reason)." "We're doing this because the curriculum says we have to (even when it never has)." "We're doing this because I think it's a crime if you don't learn it and/or read it." "We're doing this because I said so."

My dissatisfaction over these kinds of responses led to restlessness and feelings that I was not actually doing what was best for my students. I began toying with the idea that students needed more choice but they also needed to plan their own paths to success. I wanted them to start considering what kind of skills and knowledge they might need for future goals they had. I wanted them to love learning and I didn't want to continue imposing things on them that had no foundational purpose to them and that the curriculum didn't demand they know.

One day, years later, Dane stopped by my classroom for a visit. I saw him at the door, waved him in, so excited that he had decided to come back. I was eager to hear about everything he'd gone on to do. I introduced him to the class and said, "This is the *Dane* I aways talk about! You see his example assignments all the time!" Because, of course, I'd consistently used Dane's old assignments as models; he'd always done exactly what I wanted.

He walked in, cordial smile and said, "Miss, you lied to me."

I blinked. Um...what? My smile wobbled a little.

"You said I'd need to know how to do this, that, and the other thing." He gave specific examples of things I was *still* teaching to students. Things I was *still* insisting that they had to know. "And I haven't needed any of it. You. Lied."

In that moment I realized two things: One, Dane, who I thought loved me as a teacher, who I thought I'd done right by all those years ago, preparing him for success, was angry with me. He was so angry that he came back to tell me about it, in front of an audience, knowing that he'd likely embarrass me. And two, I needed to change how I was doing things because he was right: I *had* lied to him. I'd told him he would need to know so many things and forced him to complete so many tasks that ultimately were meaningless to his future. He already had a strong work ethic, he had an exemplary understanding of teamwork; in fact, he was so good at being the perfect student that he'd done everything I'd asked him to do even when I couldn't really explain why we were doing it.

He left after delivering his message. The class was stunned silent. I somehow continued teaching, mostly on autopilot, ignoring what had just happened, even though I wanted to cry.

Dane's words had been a mic drop moment. I knew, in my heart, that things were going to change in my educational life.

Dane came back a few weeks later to see me again. This time I wasn't teaching so I had time to really talk to him. I told him about plans I'd been toying with to give students more choice and voice, providing opportunities to work toward goals that they set for themselves with my guidance. He thought it was a good idea. He thought it was time for change too.

So that's what I did.

A good friend and like-minded colleague and I revamped how we planned units and lessons. We strove to put students at the centre and in control of their learning. We incorporated experiential learning and authentic tasks that actually showed how students would use their learning in the real world. We gave their learning meaning so they stopped asking, "Why are we doing this?" and we collaborated with students to work toward their goals. I've already mentioned some of the projects that came out of this new way of doing things but here are a few more:

- Students learned how to write letters of complaint for items that didn't meet expectations, then we followed through and sent them, some resulting in refunds and gift cards.
- Students tracked coupons from different organizations, collecting ones that worked in Canada, and detailed how much money could be saved and how easy they were to use, then wrote a recommendation for, or a warning against, these companies.
- We created budgets for different kinds of lifestyles.
- Students explored the best places for teens to work, surveyed students with jobs, then shared a top ten list with detailed reasons for or against different job locations.

The feedback we got was inspiring. Students told us it was the best year they'd ever had. That they had learned something *finally*. That they loved coming to school.

Did it take a lot of work? Heck, yes! I was privileged enough to have secured a grant so I could collaborate with a small team of teachers and we busted our butts to revamp how we taught. It was an entire overhaul of how we did things, and it was so worth it.

It was big — huge! — and a long time coming, but the restlessness I'd been feeling was replaced by motivation to keep changing, to keep moving forward, to keep putting students at the centre of everything I did.

Let's slow things down for a moment because it doesn't have to be go-big-or-go-home and I truly want this to be something doable for you. Baby steps.

I've given you my pie-in-the-sky version of what differentiation looks like to me. I love flying by the seat of my pants and sparking creativity and giving students choice so they have a voice in their learning. I also love being in charge and controlling everything. I've married those two things together so that my version of teaching is controlled chaos. I know what students will be doing, to a point. I know where we're headed, to a point. I know there will be surprise experiences and fails and a lot of learning. I know that some days may be overwhelming. I'm okay with that. I'm as prepared as I can be.

The outcome for students is so valuable that whatever hiccups happen are worth it to me.

But I don't want to overwhelm you before you've even started. Voice, choice, and differentiation doesn't need to be the whole shebang.

Strategy: Baby Steps to Voice, Choice, and Differentiation

- Start with a wide selection of texts that you've vetted with an anti-oppression lens and thinking about the students you have in front of you. Pick more contemporary titles and open up to different formats (audio, manga, graphic texts, manuals).
- Start with two options for products (an essay or a test, a report or a podcast, a presentation or a mini-model) for an assignment. Make sure the options are equal in preparation/process and the learning is tied to the same curriculum expectations.
- Start with a guided inquiry where you choose the question, you cultivate the research, and you control the outcome.
- Start with either/or activities: You can work on this now or work on that now.

Keep in mind that the more controlled you are with differentiation the more opportunities you have for silencing students and perpetuating oppression. Give them some variety in their day and you'll find that the students who might normally have behavioral issues start to come to class ready to learn and work. If you validate them in some way, their attitude will change, maybe not overnight but soon, I promise.

You may find that even if you're prepared for a wild west differentiated approach, your class isn't.

You may find that even if you're prepared for a wild west differentiated approach, your class isn't. The kind of scaffolding you need will depend on what the students in front of you need. They might want you to tell them what to do and how to do it, every step of the way. They haven't built up the confidence yet to take risks. They might be scared of creativity or of expressing themselves. You need to heed that and help them learn how to be confident and how to roll with mistakes and setbacks which always come with experimenting and risk-taking. Don't push them harder than they can handle; instead, work with them to achieve small successes so that you might get them to the point of exploring, discovering, and taking some chances.

Classroom Management and Student-Centred Planning

While this isn't a book about planning, I *did* say that how you plan will impact classroom management.

One of the most effective ways to win at classroom management and at teaching in general is giving students the opportunity to drive their learning by allowing them choice, giving them room to express themselves, and offering them opportunities to be creative thinkers.

That, truly, is what "real life" is about. That is how you prepare students for the future and for jobs that don't actually exist right now.

I promise you that if students feel heard, if they're able to explore their curiosities, if you work with them to succeed and they feel proud of what they accomplish, you will not have very many classroom management issues. Your students will love the learning, will look forward to it, and their self-esteem will grow.

In Short

- Giving students the opportunity to drive their learning by allowing them choice, giving them room to express themselves, and offering opportunities to be creative thinkers so they feel heard, can explore their curiosities, and achieve success will result in minimal to no classroom management issues because students will be engaged and fulfilled.
- You don't have to reinvent the wheel. Choice can be as simple as allowing a wider selection of "texts" to read or listen to. Or giving more than one option for a final product (assignment: essay or test, report or podcast; just make sure the options are equal in preparation/process and accomplish the learning of the same curriculum expectations). Or using guided inquiry where you design the question and curate the material for research.
- Behavior issues are a clue that something else is going on. It's not the behavior itself that we need to pay all attention to but the underlying catalyst. If what's going on is that you're force-feeding students work that they find meaningless, or that they don't understand, or that is boring, then of course some are going to act out.
- Don't be the teacher who says, "That's how it's always been done," or, "I had to learn it this way and I survived!" and think that's an acceptable reason to keep doing things that don't work for your students.

STEP 7

Surprise! Troubleshooting

Let's keep in mind that any disruptive behavior from a student is a cry for help. It's a canary in the coalmine. It's a warning that something is wrong.

Sometimes, a behavioral outburst only needs to be ignored in order to be defused. Sometimes, you must pick your battles because letting one little thing slip might prevent something bigger from happening. Sometimes, it's your fault because you've said or done something that has hurt a student emotionally or psychologically. Sometimes, it's not you — the student is going through something outside of your scope of awareness.

Keep in mind that something as simple as a transition can be hard for some students and they may become dysregulated by change of routine or moving from an activity they enjoy to one they don't. Others may become overstimulated by something (games, recess, etc). You need to plan ahead for this or at least anticipate this might happen and have some backup go-tos that will help limit these escalation triggers.

Make sure you are giving ample warning of a transition. Use some kind of signal, have an established routine, or have a transition activity to help students prepare for moving from one activity to the next. Maybe it's a stretch or a tour around the classroom. Maybe it's a signal like turning the lights on or off. Something that clearly marks a break from one activity to another

Knowing that, let's first and foremost work on tempering our reactions to behavior that seems inappropriate for the environment. Let's work on calm reactions and neutral responses. Escalation often happens because we fail to remain calm.

In every case I've listed in the next few pages, if you follow my suggestions and the student escalates anyway, you can always call for backup from Admin or another teacher and you should also contact home later to bring parents/guardians up to date.

The first step in any reaction is to see if the student will tell you what's wrong or if you can use contextual clues to figure out what the problem is. If you learn what the problem is, then you can try to help the student in a more specific way.

You also want to intervene early — as soon as you notice something is off, step in. Don't wait to see what will happen; that can turn into a gotcha very quickly. If you know ahead of time that a student will be triggered by something, don't do it, or remove the student from the situation before they're triggered.

Avoid embarrassing students by calling them out or punishing them with shame. This should be self-explanatory. If you shame someone, they're going to react in some way. Could be tears, could be self-hatred, could be anger. It's terrible to do to someone and doesn't achieve what you think it does. No lesson is learned about the behavior you want to curb; instead, students learn not to trust you.

Teach students the acceptable ways to deal with overwhelming emotion. Teach thinking before acting. Work with students on a process of slowing down when impulsive behavior tempts them and teach them to ask themselves: What am I doing? What should I be doing?

You can use lessons to help them control breathing or count to ten before reacting. You can teach them about grounding and being in the moment, noticing three things they can hear, two things they can see, one thing they can feel. You can give them outs, designated areas of the classroom that a student can move to when feeling overwhelmed without having to ask permission.

Teacher self-reflection needs to come with any behavior issue as well. Whether it's in the moment and you are able to examine the last few minutes of what you said or did, or if it's later that day or the next day, you must consider how you may have played a role in what happened. There have been times where I've gone home angry about something only to realize later that I was the one who picked a fight instead of deescalating a situation. It usually happens over something that I feel very strongly about but obviously the student doesn't. Over my career, I've had to adjust what my absolute non-negotiables are so that I'm not enforcing a rule that is unfair simply because I don't want a rule to be broken or because I want to save face in front of other students and teachers. As I said, I like to be in control and, at times, that turns me into an impenetrable wall, if only because "How dare you?!" or "The Audacity!"

So, with every situation I list below, I suggest always:

- First-time violation: give a reminder of the rules and your expectations.
- Second-time violation: give another reminder but also name a consequence that will happen if you have to repeat yourself again.
- Third-time violation: follow through on the consequence.

Following these three steps works for me because it's succinct and doesn't drag things out. Students also tend to understand the count of three. Three strikes, you're out. Three little pigs. "I'm going to count to three!"

To be totally honest with you, I'm not a fan of lists like the one I'm about to give you because it seems like an if/then situation when you're dealing with classroom management. If a student does this, then you do that. It's not really how classroom management works. Each student and each behavior is unique, even when it seems as if you see the same behavior over and over again. I dislike approaching any situation with a strategy locked and loaded and prefer to work a situation with my natural skills.

In my opinion, it's better to be proactive rather than reactive.

Actually, I prefer to prevent behavior from happening in the first place.

That being said, it took me a long time to hone my natural classroom management skills and I would have killed to have some kind of go-to list to help me at the beginning of my career.

Luckily for you, I knew one day I'd be writing this book. I've been collecting advice from teachers over the years. I've written down situations that I've heard about, that teacher-friends and family have vented about. I've curated ideas that I've gotten from self-help strategies to psychological studies, and from my own experiences and have figured out how to apply them to common situations that happen in classrooms. In fact, anytime I read or watch anything, I'm mining it for classroom management ideas.

Some of the ideas you'll find below are "common sense" and some I've already talked about in this book. These ideas transcend age and grade and should be applicable no matter where or when you're teaching with one caveat: kindergarten is its own world and requires a unique kind of expertise that I won't pretend to have. The following are some ideas that might help you in a pinch when dealing with classroom disruptions but I'd like to caution that prevention is much better than reaction.

What If?

A STUDENT REFUSES TO DO WHAT YOU'VE ASKED THEM TO DO.

- Consider if the task you're asking them to do is too easy, boring, inappropriate, or triggering in some way.
- Find out why they're refusing. If they have a good reason, then come up with something else they can do that will meet both of your needs.
- Give a choice of reasonable actions and be firm: "You can do this or that, your choice. What will it be?"
- If they argue, simply restate the options with a rationale for the choices you're offering, stressing that they must pick one.
- If they still refuse, you might need to send them to the office. Make sure to call ahead to let them know whom you're sending, why and what your expectations are. "I'm sending Cam because he's refusing to do any work. I'm concerned that something is going on that he won't share with me. I'd like Mrs. VP to speak to him please."

A STUDENT LEAVES CLASS WITHOUT PERMISSION.

- Remind the student of expectations for leaving class, privately and calmly.
- Ask the student why they left. See if you can come up with a solution together that works better for both of you — they might be overstimulated or bored or have physical needs that require they leave class.
- You could try writing up a contract with the student, although it's rare that a student will care about a piece-of-paper commitment.
- Incentivize with an age-appropriate reward (not candy) to encourage consistent desired behavior. Find their currency and use it to help them learn how to follow the rules. You're not bribing, you're redirecting by offering a motivator that will encourage the student to do what you want them to do. It's a reward for achieving a goal, which can be something as simple as saying something kind or having time to color.
- You can make a deal with the student to give you a signal when they need to leave. Then follow up with them once they're back. Consequences need to be applied if trust is broken so if a student takes advantage of this deal, then they may lose privileges for a time.

- You might have a system for the whole class where they achieve points for some bigger goal. I caution you, though: using this method is okay as long as you're not using the system to punish. You're not going to take points away. You're not going to use them to shame. You're going to pay attention and if a student is falling behind in points, you're going to do something to help them achieve more points and catch up. We don't want anyone to feel they're losing in ways that they can't dig out from.

A STUDENT IS NOT PARTICIPATING IN AN ACTIVITY.

- Offer different options that will include the student but not pressure them into participating. Maybe they don't want to speak but will type. Maybe they don't want to stand but will sit. Maybe they just need time to decompress because they're upset about something. Maybe they need the bouncy chair to think.
- You can tap into something you know they have an interest in and make a quick switch so the activity is more appealing to them. I once had a student who really loved Trolls (the movie characters) and often, if she was struggling to participate, I would ask her what the Trolls would do. Or I would prompt her to make her response with Trolls as the topic.
- You can also give the student a special role such as a leadership opportunity, some kind of privilege that motivates them to model for the class.
- You can ask if they'd be willing to help another student with the activity.
- If the student really doesn't want to engage with anyone else, that's okay too. They can work on something else or do the activity in their own way.
- You may need to revisit this with the student (and possibility with parents/guardians) later — explain to the student what you need them to show you in order to achieve a particular goal and figure out how to do that together in a way that's comfortable for the student.
- You can provide clear timelines and chunk work into manageable tasks as a way of prevention
- You can make sure students understand that whatever isn't done can be done later (maybe during catch-up time but not for homework — that will seem like a punishment).

A STUDENT GETS PHYSICAL WHEN EMOTIONS RUN HIGH.

- The first time this happens, calmly clear the room. Evacuate other students from the room and call for backup.
- Going forward, or as prevention, if you already know a student reacts this way:
  - Make adjustments to reduce stress: avoid triggers, have a tight schedule, reduce stimulating activities.
  - If you sense something is off, position yourself near the student. Sometimes proximity is enough of a signal to prevent an unwanted behavior from escalating.
  - Teach students how to overcome heightened emotions. Give them a set of steps to follow if they're feeling upset. Maybe they can hand you a note or a picture card, or leave a note or card on a specific corner of their desk to alert you when they are upset. Or maybe they can move to a calming space in the classroom — no questions asked.

A STUDENT BLAMES OTHERS FOR THEIR OWN MISTAKES.

- Teach about taking responsibility and normalize making mistakes.
- Teach some problem-solving strategies for when things don't work out the way we've planned and model apologies. You can do this with role-play, where students have a short and simple script to follow so they can practice reactions to failure or setback or losing. You can also teach them a mantra to say, like, "We can learn from this," or, "It's not over, yet," or, "There's always a next time."
- Focus on the positive and give encouraging feedback when you see the student taking responsibility for something.
- Set some boundaries or guidelines around some of the more egregious excuses that won't fly for you. Name them. For example, "Please don't say, 'It wasn't my fault'; instead say, 'This is what happened.'"
- Don't argue with a student who refuses to take responsibility; consider the truth behind their excuses — as outlandish as it may sound, they might be telling the truth.
- Last resort: remove the student from the activity until they accept responsibility. Be prepared for escalation.

A STUDENT BLAMES THEMSELVES FOR EVERY LITTLE THING.

- Teach about perfectionism and reflection and what it means to be too hard on oneself.
- Offer sincere praise often.
- Avoid activities that create competition.
- Be clear with expectations and set boundaries around negative self-talk.
- Model making mistakes and redefine failure as a bump in the road and a necessary part of the learning process.
- Place less emphasis on grades.
- Direct students to use the word "yet" when failure occurs. "I don't know how to multiply fractions, yet".

Keep in mind that the human brain continues to develop well into our twenties — so, you're dealing with people who maybe don't yet have the wiring to consider consequences, "rational" thoughts, or empathy. You also may be dealing with people who will never develop those brain connections due to natural developmental impacts as well as environmental impacts. What that means is that you need to practice patience and understanding when dealing with students and know that you might need to remind or correct the same student every day about something because they are not yet able to encode it into their brains.

A STUDENT DAMAGES SCHOOL MATERIAL/PROPERTY.

- Explain expectations for use of property/school supplies.
- Reenforce acceptable use with praise/reward.
- Supervise with vigilance.
- Follow through on consequences.
- Limit use of material.
- Escalate to administration/contact home.

A STUDENT WILL NOT FOLLOW CLASSROOM RULES.

- Consider working with students to create classroom rules so they feel ownership over them.

- Discuss the "whys" behind the rules and make sure those "whys" make sense.
- Quietly address when a rule is broken and follow through on consequences that have been established. Make sure the consequences match the crime.
- Give choices to redirect a student, options that prevent the student from totally refusing to obey. For instance, if a student is refusing to stay seated during a lesson then offer them the option to sit on the bouncy chair or to stand as long as they don't bother anyone.
- Work with the student on consequences that will work for them.
- Make sure rules are posted so students can see them all the time.
- Reinforce when the student shows the desired behavior: "Thank you for following our rules today, Patrick".

A STUDENT CONSTANTLY INTERRUPTS.

- Teach, then practice, communication strategies and soft skills focusing on conversation conventions.
- Make sure you are modeling conscientious communication with students. Do not just break in, instead use phrases like, "I'm sorry to interrupt,." or, "Do you mind if I jump in here?"
- Have a signal that the student knows means, "Stop interrupting."
- Give the student paper to jot down ideas instead of interrupting.
- Educate yourself about ADHD. Talk with students about impulsive urges and think up ways to keep impulses from taking over. Maybe sharing ideas with a seat partner quietly or writing a note or taking a walk around the room without disturbing others would help.
- Give positive reinforcement when the student is displaying appropriate behavior.

A STUDENT DOESN'T WORK WELL IN GROUPS.

- Teach students about teamwork and collaboration.
- Modify activity so the student can work alone.
- Find out what motivates the student to act the way they do in groups. See if there are ways to prevent the behavior or ways to teach alternative coping methods.
- Give choice of groups or at least allow buddies to stick together in groups.
- Give the student a leadership role. Teach students what it means to be a good leader, then offer the leadership to the student who is struggling. Better yet, use a co-leader approach so two students have each other to bounce ideas off while they're leading.
- Teach students how to resolve conflicts in a group.

A STUDENT REFUSES TO SPEAK IN FRONT OF CLASS.

- Show compassion — don't force a student to speak.
- Show interest in the student and learn what stops them from speaking.
- Offer alternative ways to participate (online chat, sticky notes, speaking buddy).
- Start with low-risk activities like speaking quietly with a partner or small group.
- Develop goals with the student about speaking publicly and reward them when the goals are accomplished.

A STUDENT DOESN'T WAIT THEIR TURN.

- Teach the class about taking turns. What does it mean? What does it look like? How do we do it? Why do we do it?
- Use an object to indicate when it's time for a turn (pass the object to the person who is next).
- Have clear expectations and directions for taking turns (e.g., put hand up, wait until called on).
- Have students teach others what they've learned about taking turns (could be a younger grade or someone at home).
- Remind the student privately before an activity about your expectations for taking turns.
- Have clear consequences, such as that the student may be asked to sit out the next round.
- Supervise and be aware/attentive so you can prevent issues from cropping up ahead of time.

A STUDENT MOVES TOO QUICKLY FROM ONE ACTIVITY TO ANOTHER.

- Use a timer and redirect the student back to task.
- Give feedback to ensure a task is completed; if not, ask the student to fix the issues pointed out in the feedback.
- Offer enrichment if the task is too easy.
- Give the student a checklist to show completion. Make sure it's chunked into manageable steps.
- Avoid competitive tasks or an atmosphere that creates competition. Avoid saying, "Whoever finishes first wins!" Unless you want students to rush.
- Remind all students what the steps are to clean up after each task before moving to the next.
- Have clear expectations for what to do when an activity is done.

A STUDENT WON'T STAY SEATED.

- Include breaks in work time, lead stretching activities with the class, or allow walking around the room.
- Give the student a quiet space away from others to work, get up, stretch, etc.
- Give clear instructions about not disturbing others and what to do if they're feeling restless.
- Ask the student to count to ten when the urge to get up strikes, and see if that helps them move past the impulse.
- Have fidget toys available to redirect energy.
- Create a norm for thinking circles (any student can get up and walk a circle around the classroom to think).
- Use flexible seating so students can move freely.
- Designate times when students shouldn't be walking around (e.g., when you are teaching).
- Provide choices of activities or alternative activities to switch to for a brain refresh.
- Consider if the task is boring or too easy.

A STUDENT IS OFF TASK/NOT READY FOR TASK/DOESN'T USE TIME WELL.

- Teach, then reinforce, steps to readiness. What do we need? Where can we find it? Do we have all of our supplies? What do we start with first? What comes next?
- Help the student understand how to build and use checklists.
- Make sure the student fully grasps what the task is and what they're supposed to be doing.
- Allow extra time and make sure the student understands that they have extra time available if needed.
- Find an organization strategy that works for the student. Maybe they have their own supply of materials in a cubby. Maybe they use their phone to set time limits.
- Chunk activities into manageable steps.
- Use a buddy system to check for readiness. "Please check with your buddy and give a thumbs up if you're ready to start."
- Have a routine for readiness. "First we..." "Then we..." "Next we..."
- Use a timer for the class so they know how long they have.
- Gamify readiness — use a points system for students so they are rewarded when they're ready to go and on task.
- Make a list for students to follow so they know what tools they need for a particular task.
- Redirect the student to the task: tap desk, quietly remind, share a post-it note with directions.
- Make a deal: work for five minutes, rest for two.
- Limit unstructured time so students don't get into a rut of doing nothing.
- Separate a student from peers who encourage them to be off task. This includes changing a seating plan if necessary.

A STUDENT DOESN'T COMPLETE HOMEWORK OR ASSIGNMENTS ON TIME.

- Have students complete work in class and make sure homework has a purpose and is not assigned out of spite or as punishment.
- Find out what might prevent a student from completing work at home. Could be lack of technology or wifi. Could be family obligations like babysitting. Could be extracurricular sports or groups.
- Use flexible deadlines and allow students to hand in work at different times depending on individual needs.
- Reconsider the amount of work and purpose of homework (it's for practice and oftentimes practice is better done with the teacher available to help).
- Teach all students how to use checklists and calendars/agenda.
- Chunk tasks with shorter due dates to make the work more palatable.

A teacher friend recently shared a powerful story with me about the "ah-ha" moment she had that changed how she viewed her students, homework, and missing deadlines.

As a secondary English teacher, she was used to students blowing off assignments until the last minute and coming up with a variety of stories to explain why they didn't prioritize their English assignment above other assignments. When one of her students asked to speak to her privately after being absent from class (and scheduled work periods) for days, then missing an assignment due date, she was ready to lay into him about responsibility and time management.

What she wasn't ready for was this:

"I'm so sorry I missed the due date for the essay, Miss," he said, tears beginning to form.

The tears immediately caught her off guard. This wasn't a student who openly shared emotion. It was a student who was usually a little contrary with teachers.

"I, uh, got kicked out of my house the other night and I have nowhere to live right now and I'm staying with a friend but her mom isn't cool with me being there so I don't know where I'm gonna go. But, I promise, I'll hand the essay in as soon as I figure out what to do."

In that moment, my friend realized that the English essay, which had seemed so important a few seconds before, was meaningless in the face of homelessness.

In that moment, she decided that she wasn't going to hold the courses she taught above compassion.

"You know what, Tyler?" she said. "Let's not worry about the essay. Let's figure out a way to help you get through this."

And that's what she did.

You have no idea what a student might be going through.

You have no idea what a student might be going through. Every moment of every day something out of their control can impact their lives in profound ways.

A STUDENT TALKS CONSTANTLY DURING CLASS.

- Teach students about active listening and how to be present in the moment.
- Give the student time for talking.
- Build in a social time during activities.
- Figure out if it's avoidance or defiance and find ways to reengage the student to work. They may not understand or they may use talking as a way of thinking.
- Ask the student if they'd like to work in a quiet space away from friends.
- Teach students about self-awareness and how to notice when something is preventing them from accomplishing their goals.

A STUDENT DOESN'T COOPERATE WITH A SUPPLY TEACHER.

- Have clear expectations for students when you are away. Talk to them ahead of time so they understand what you expect. Give a heads-up about an upcoming absence if possible.
- Assign duties to students to help the supply. (Not attendance! That's a privacy breach.) Assign a student to show the supply teacher around the room. Assign someone else to distribute books. Assign someone else to do whatever duties you do on a daily basis.
- Make sure the supply teacher is aware of rules and routines.
- Leave enough work that is engaging and has purpose.
- Give the supply teacher some ideas about how to establish rapport with students. Give an overview of class atmosphere.
- Give suggestions for recourse if students are misbehaving.
- Involve students in planning for a supply teacher visit. Perhaps teach them about being a cordial host.

I just heard a story about the flip side to this. A student who normally had many behavioral issues was the "perfect" student for a supply teacher. The supply teacher claimed that the student helped her without asking and was very pleasant to talk to, didn't break any rules, and overall was not even a blip on her radar for behavior concerns. The regular classroom teacher was baffled since her experience with the student was the complete opposite. He was defiant, spoke harshly to her, and was often sent to the office for discipline. My observation of this scenario reflects back to the parts of this book that ask teachers to consider the role they may play in a student's behavior. I'm not saying it's the teacher's fault that the student has behavior issues in her presence. What this tells me is that this student is behaving in a certain way for certain reasons. Not that helpful, I know, but think about it…if the student can turn the behavior disruptions off then there must be a trigger that turns them on. What are the triggers? Is the student desperate for a chance to reinvent himself? Do personalities clash with the regular teacher? Is it the work that is often left when the regular teacher is away? Getting to the bottom of why a student would behave so differently with a stranger could be life-changing for both the regular classroom teacher and the student.

A STUDENT LIES ALL THE TIME, OFTEN FOR WEIRD REASONS.

Some of the commons ones I've heard lately are: lying about missing work — "You never gave it to me." "I handed it in. You must have lost it." Or lying about where they just were — "I wasn't in the library" — but you've seen them walk out of the library. "I'm not eating." Their jaw is working pretty hard on air then. Or "I don't have a pencil." There's one in plain view in their open pencil case. My favorite, "I have a spare." But they don't. What to do?

- Increase opportunities for success and positive reinforcement.
- Don't push for information sharing or explanation, which may force the student to lie in order to save face.
- Make it okay to be forgetful and to make mistakes; lies happen when the stakes are too high and a student becomes overwhelmed.
- Teach students how to manage time and prove to students that you can be trusted to be kind and flexible if mistakes are made.
- Don't act if you don't have all the facts — making assumptions about truthfulness can lead to a loss of trust. It might sound like a wild tale but it could be true. Make sure you have evidence to support your assertions.
- Give second and third chances.

A STUDENT IGNORES CONSEQUENCES.

- Consequences must be consistently applied in every instance for every student unless there are extenuating circumstances.
- Appropriate behavior requires positive reinforcement. If you see a student following a rule or stopping themselves from breaking a rule, point it out (privately) and thank them.
- Limit situations where a student may be overwhelmed or overstimulated to prevent unwanted behavior.
- Natural consequences may be that the student no longer gets to participate in an activity.
- Teach about consequences and cause and effect.
- Give choice to minimize backing a student into a corner.
- Intervene early.

A STUDENT MAKES INAPPROPRIATE, CRITICAL, OR DEROGATORY REMARKS ABOUT OTHERS.

- Intervene immediately. Do not ignore this situation. Calmly move into the scene and address what's going on and what has been said. Not only is this important for the student who is making the comment, but it's equally so for the students who are watching. You are going to model what it means to be a responsible bystander.

- Do not embarrass a student by calling them out. Private conversations are better than public shaming.
- Natural consequences may apply here. Other students may move away from the student so they are not associated. They might start to avoid that student. Help all students to reflect on what natural consequences are and what they mean. Teach students how to repair broken friendships.
- Teach students how to express their opinions without attacking someone else.
- Teach all students how to communicate with others and set clear boundaries about words that are mean and hurtful.
- Teach students how to be responsible bystanders.
- Use the situation as a teaching moment but do it in a way that isn't judgemental. Try to help the student understand what it would be like for someone to say that to them or how what they've said hurts other people.
- Teach the student about social awareness and how to express their feelings in socially acceptable ways.

A STUDENT MAKES INAPPROPRIATE NOISES.

- Ignore the noises — as annoying as they are, not giving attention sometimes defuses the impulse.
- Privately ask the student what the noises are all about.
- Use proximity to discourage noises — standing close to the student might be enough to get them to stop.
- Quietly remind the student of classroom expectations.
- Reinforce positive behavior from the student.
- Ask the student to raise their hand if they have something to contribute.
- Give the entire class a moment to make noises and get it out of their systems.
- Teach the student how to ground themselves (noticing/naming three things they see, two things they feel, one thing they hear) to redirect impulsive behavior.
- Do not encourage the student by laughing, unless you want it to become a thing that happens all the time.
- Have consequences like not allowing the student to move on to the next activity (which they like) until the noises stop.
- Reduce the amount of time students are sitting and listening to you and/or having to work quietly.
- Reduce stimulation — lower lights if possible, close blinds, stop computer work, turn off music, etc.
- Use a signal to alert the student to be quiet.

A STUDENT DOESN'T TAKE CONSTRUCTIVE CRITICISM.

- Teach students about feedback — its purpose and how to use it. Tie it into activities so students can practice giving and receiving. Be sure to stress that we all learn by making mistakes.

- Remove the student from their group/partnership and one-on-one teach them about constructive criticism. Remind them of the appropriate responses to constructive criticism.
- Teach the student how to self-critique effectively.
- Be positive in your approach and offer support so the student achieves success.
- Use compliments on either side of criticisms. "You did a fantastic job with your inquiry questions. You need to do more research for this part and that part because you don't have enough evidence yet. Your voice comes through in this area so well."
- Make sure there is a lot of practice time for any task to build confidence.
- Understand that sometimes students are taking criticism so personally that it isn't about the work as much as it is about their self-esteem. Spend time building their self-esteem and they'll be more open to criticism.

A STUDENT AGITATES AND PROVOKES OTHERS WHO ARE TRYING TO WORK.

- Build in breaks so the student can get their energy out.
- Remind students that they shouldn't bother others who are working.
- Redirect the student to a different activity to keep them occupied.
- Check in with the student, review work, and offer feedback so the student can work on corrections.
- Have enrichment activities ready for students who get work done quickly.
- Ask students "who would like some help?", then ask the disruptive student to sit with another student to help them complete a task.
- Set goals with the student for not bothering others who are working and reward them when they reach their goals.
- Assign appealing duties to the student to get done while others are finishing up their work.

A STUDENT TOUCHES PEOPLE WITHOUT CONSENT OR GETS INTO THEIR SPACE.

- Determine if this is due to overstimulation; if so, redirect to a calmer activity/area of the room.
- Teach all students about personal space and consent. Include phrases to be used like, "Hands to ourselves," "We don't touch others," or, "Stay in your bubble." Encourage students to use the phrasing when they see someone who needs a reminder.
- Use positive reinforcement for not touching others. "I love how you got Cael's attention without touching her, James!)
- Reduce the number of situations in which a student could come into contact with others.
- Consider your own actions. Are you modeling asking for consent?
- Put the student closer to you for more direct supervision.
- Try to intervene early, not after physical contact has been made.

A STUDENT DOESN'T FOLLOW VERBAL INSTRUCTIONS/FAILS TO FOLLOW STEPS.

- Make sure you have the student's attention before speaking.
- Reduce distractions ("Phones down, eyes on me").
- Give enough time for each step.
- Check in to ensure understanding.

- Be clear when giving instructions. Follow a sequence. Follow up with written instructions. Use pictures and diagrams.
- Chunk instructions into manageable bites and set timelines for completion.
- Ask a student helper to write instructions on the board as you're giving them.
- Check in with parents/guardians regarding hearing/eyesight to make sure there are no medical issues.
- Ask the student to repeat directions (privately) as they understand them and give positive reinforcement.
- Follow up verbal instructions with one-on-one directions to reinforce sequence and expectations.
- Stand close to the student when giving instructions.
- Teach active listening skills.

A STUDENT AVOIDS DOING WORK.

- Make sure the student understands what is being asked.
- Work with the student to ensure understanding.
- Engage the student with topics of interest.
- Plan alternative activities.
- Give time limits and breaks.
- Give positive feedback.
- Try to understand what and why work is being avoided. Is it boring? Seems irrelevant? Just not the most important thing to the student?
- Help the student understand consequences of not completing work. Be honest, realistic, and compassionate. Avoid lying or making something seem more important than it is.
- Plan a schedule to catch up on missing work.
- Chunk instructions and set deadlines for each part.

A STUDENT ISN'T MOTIVATED BY REWARDS.

- Take time to figure out what the student's currency is.
- Engage the student with tasks that are interesting, then reinforce with positive praise.
- Work on self-esteem by ensuring small successes daily.
- Ask them to teach you something about a subject that interests them or something they recently learned. Be curious with them: "How good is Google Read and Write at recording our voices? Let's see."
- Encourage them to design their own learning or give alternative suggestions for something they want to learn.
- Play a game with them, something low-key competitive like an online typing game to see who can type faster.
- Give a leadership role or responsibility; make sure it matters.

A STUDENT IS CHEATING OR PLAGIARIZING.

- Clearly outline what constitutes cheating/plagiarizing and what the consequences are.
- Teach students how to avoid cheating/plagiarizing, how to study for and how to write tests, how to cite work properly.
- Follow through on consequences. You may have a school rule/policy about this so be sure to check there first. You can ask the student to redo

the assignment. You can ask them to redo the parts that are plagiarized or where they cheated. You might give a zero (although that means you're at best assigning a grade for nothing or at worst assigning a grade for a behavior.)

- Remove opportunities for dishonest conduct; bags, books, and notebooks away, phones turned off, smart watches in pockets, scientific calculators/calculators with a memory put away.
- Supervise at all times.
- Use regular check-ins with assignments.
- Use work periods for in-class supervision rather than sending students home to work.
- Probe for truth rather than hammering with accusations. "I'm wondering where you got this idea from? I don't see a citation here. How come?" Instead of, "I know you and Kelsey copied from one another." or, "You have the exact same answers as Walid."
- Allow for flexible timelines and teacher feedback.
- Find out the cause: it could be that the student doesn't understand, is unprepared, is anxious, is scared of failure, etc.
- Put more emphasis on process rather than on one-shot/timed final product.

A STUDENT THROWS TEMPER TANTRUMS.

- Sometimes you need to let that tantrum run its course. Make sure the student and those around them are safe but let it ride.
- Try to prevent it from happening by intervening early when you see a student escalating.
- Learn the student's triggers and avoid them.
- If necessary, call for backup and clear the room of other students.
- Show compassion and ask what you can do to help.
- Offer a prearranged alternative setting or calming activity.
- Figure out, with the student, how to avoid tantrums and put a sequence in place that's easy to remember so the student can time themselves out before they fully escalate.

A STUDENT USES INAPPROPRIATE LANGUAGE.

- Remove the student from the interaction or remove the other students from the situation.
- Reinforce when the student is using appropriate language.
- Establish rules of acceptable behavior and language.
- Teach students about appropriate language and time and place for language as well as alternative ways to express emotions: darn, heck, poop, or even silly words like balderdash, crikey, drat!
- Allow natural consequences such as isolation from peers but follow up with a conversation with the student to help them make the connection between the behavior and the way peers are reacting and teach them how to repair the damage.
- Separate the student from others who might be encouraging the language.
- Ask the student to keep a tally of the times they feel like swearing — this will hopefully bring awareness to when and why, which could help you guide the student to more neutral responses.

- Consider reducing activities that might lead to overstimulation.
- Be calm when addressing the student; do not bring attention, as that might be why the swearing is happening. In fact, sometimes you should just ignore it as it's only meant to get a reaction.

Some Extra Cautions

Some behaviors are linked to undiagnosed exceptionalities and may show up in different ways depending on many factors: restlessness, impulsivity, crying, confusion, no eye contact, perseverating, blurted words or noises. Please make sure you have some grasp of common exceptionalities such as ADHD, OCD, autism, anxiety, and depression.

If a student deliberately hurts themselves or animals, destroys teacher's/classmates'/their own materials, regularly sleeps/is exceptionally tired in class, sets fires or brings weapons to school (don't scoff, each of these things has happened in a classroom near you), physically fights with others, or threatens others, then you must get backup. Do not try to deal with this on your own. You must notify your administration and/or call for help. You must notify appropriate social services under the direction of your administration. Parents/guardians need to be made aware and must be part of the plan for help but discussing it with them might be a job for your administration or a crisis team rather than you alone. In any of these extreme situations, you need to escalate the response to your boss(es) because they are trained to deal with it. Don't try to handle it by yourself.

- You must not get in the middle of a fight or put your hands on a student to stop a fight. No matter how much you are compelled to do so, stay back and keep other students safe, evacuate the area, or go to find help. Inserting yourself can result in injury to you or someone else, and it could lead to disciplinary action that will impact your future career and/or even criminal charges.
- Do not take it upon yourself to search a student's bag or personal items. This is above your pay grade and should be handled by Admin and the police. If you suspect a student is carrying something dangerous or illegal, make your admin aware and let them handle it with the necessary next steps. If they refuse to handle it, call your union and call the police.
- Do not lock a student in a room to contain them and do not try to physically stop them from leaving your room.
- Do not manhandle a student to get them moving.
- If you smell alcohol or something else on a student, notify the principal rather than accusing the student or drawing attention to it.
- If you see an intruder in the building, notify administration.

I know that these strategies will not help in any situation where a teacher is being abused, physically assaulted, bullied, or stalked and their cries for help are being dismissed or ignored by unions and/or employers. If this is you, I encourage you to call the police and file a complaint or press charges. No one should have to live with that kind of treatment in or outside of any work environment.

Epilogue: This Is the End

There are people who know me as a teacher, colleagues I've worked with who might be reading this book thinking, there is no way this is what Angie does. In fact, when I was transitioning from teaching to consulting a few years ago, the speech that was given at my farewell party was about what a paradox I am.

What the speech giver said was that my students were so well behaved that if you walked into my class they'd be working away, unbothered by the intrusion, not a behavior out of place, which suggested that they were scared of me or that I reigned with an iron fist. It would suggest that I must be militaristic to have them in line all the time. But the paradox, for the speech giver, was that my students weren't scared at all. They were so enthusiastic about how much they loved being in my classes. When asked, they said I was fair but didn't take any crap. That I had high expectations and helped them do well. Students requested me to be their teacher and demanded to be let into my classes. True story: one summer, a student was with family in Pakistan and found out she would not be in my class the following September. She recounted to me later how she had called and called until someone at the school called her back and that she made sure she was in my class. She'd told me that I was the only teacher who had ever understood her and let her be who she wanted to be.

At my farewell party, the speech giver said I had a fan base — one that was so large and authentic, spanning years of teaching, that I couldn't possibly be a tyrant and I was obviously doing something right.

I didn't know until I heard the speech (which made me sob like a baby) that anyone else noticed those things about me. I felt validated and seen and a little embarrassed by the attention.

There's no secret to how I achieve that level of devotion and collaboration in my classrooms. It's no mystery to me, at least not any more. I know teachers who have the same philosophy and the same success and do the same things to achieve the same outcomes.

You can replicate what I do. Just follow the steps I've covered in this book.

If you set expectations, are fair but firm, genuinely care about your students, and help them succeed, then you'll rarely have classroom management issues and yes, you'll develop a fan base who come back years later to visit and actually say really nice things about you, like what a positive impact you've had on their lives.

Like everything else in teaching, developing classroom management skills is an evolutionary process. It's not going to happen overnight. It takes time, patience, and trial and error.

I wish you all the best in creating the classroom of your dreams, and I am so grateful that you have included me, my thoughts, and my experiences in your journey.

Acknowledgements

This project came with a lot of imposter syndrome. Who do you think you are, Angie Barrett? Writing a book about classroom management? Leave it to the experts.

My inner voice is a harsh critic.

When I tentatively began telling people that I was writing a book about classroom management, my friends, family, and colleagues all had the same reaction: it's about time!

So, thank you to the usual suspects: my kids, Teagan and Warren, my husband, Yendor, my mom and dad, Marie and Virg Minchella, who are biased, yes, but whose support I always know I can count on.

Thank you to my cousin, Leslie Leamen-Denier, who knew, way before I did, that I needed to write this book. To my family and friends in education, Andi LeBlanc, Jen Chu, Kristy and Mike Damtsis, Michelle Anderton, Beverly Woodfine, Anna Sotiropoulos and Frank Minchella, who shared stories with me over the years about their experiences in and out of the classroom. Also, Aunt Jayne, you keep my do-right radar doing right. To all the teachers, EAs, and support staff I've worked with who have helped shape my understanding of classroom management, thank you!

To Michelle von Enckevort and Laura MacGillivray for reading an early draft, boosting my confidence, and echoing my beliefs. I've learned so much from you both over the years.

To my mentors, Nadia Bearcroft and Derrick Schellenberg: it's been twenty years, if you can believe it, and I'm still learning from the example you both set.

To my wonderful publisher, Mary Macchiusi for helping me fulfill a career-long dream and to David Kilgour, my editor, for helping me get this manuscript into shape. A million times, thank you!

Thanks to Theresa Meikle for being the reason I approached Pembroke Publishers in the first place and for supporting my ideas right from the start.

To every student I've ever interacted with, thank you for helping me grow as a teacher, for being patient with my flaws, and understanding of the learning journey I continue on.

Finally, thank you, dear readers, for picking up this book and, at the very least, reading this acknowledgement page. It is my hope that you've also flipped through the pages and have taken a gem or two from my ideas. I've love to hear from you, good or bad, as a review, an email, or on social media, so please don't hesitate to reach out.

Works Cited

Crane, D., and Kauffman, M. (Producers). (1994-2004). *Friends* [TV series]. Bright/Kauffman/Crane Productions; NBC.

Ontario Government, Ministry of Education. "Growing success: assessment, evaluation, and reporting in Ontario's schools, kindergarten to Grade 12." *Ontario.ca*, Ontario, 29 June 2022, https://www.ontario.ca/page/growing-success-assessment-evaluation-and-reporting-ontario-schools-kindergarten-grade-12#section-0. Accessed 10 September 2025.

Ontario Government, Ministry of Education. "Language (2023)." *Curriculum and Resources*,

Ontario, 2023, https://www.dcp.edu.gov.on.ca/en/curriculum/elementary-language. Accessed 10 September 2025.

Ontario Government, Ministry of Education. "Mathematics." *Mathematics*, Ontario, 2020, https://www.dcp.edu.gov.on.ca/en/curriculum/elementary-mathematics. Accessed 10 September 2025.

Index